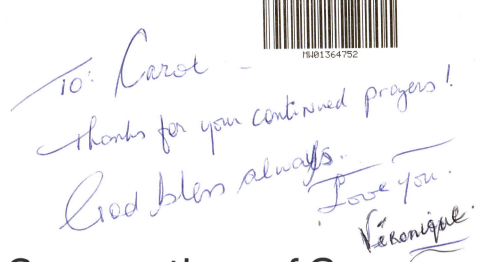

Conversations of Grace

Testimonies of Blessings, Faith, Miracles and Courage

By Bramalea Free Methodist Church

Edited by Angela J. Carter

Conversations of Grace:
Testimonies of Blessings, Faith, Miracles and Courage

Copyright © 2016 Bramalea Free Methodist Church

All Rights Reserved. No part of this publication may be reproduced, stored in a retrieval system, or transmitted in any form by any means, electronic, mechanical, photocopying, recording or otherwise, without written permission from the author, except for brief quotations embodied in critical articles or reviews.

For information on book purchases please write:
Bramalea Free Methodist Church
355 Howden Boulevard
Brampton, ON, L6S 4L6

Library and Archives Canada Cataloguing in Publication

Conversations of grace : testimonies of blessings, faith, miracles and courage / Bramalea Free Methodist Church ; edited by Angela J. Carter.

Includes bibliographical references.
Issued in print and electronic formats.
ISBN 978-0-9951531-0-3 (paperback).--ISBN 978-0-9951531-2-7 (html).--ISBN 978-0-9951531-1-0 (pdf)

1. Faith. 2. Miracles. 3. Courage. 4. God.
I. Carter, Angela J., editor II. Bramalea Free Methodist Church, author, issuing body

BV4637.C67 2016   234'.23   C2016-905005-X
                                              C2016-907352-1

COVER DESIGN: Jasmine A Rock
Interior formatting & layout: Hemant Lal
All Scripture quotations, unless otherwise indicated, are taken from
THE HOLY BIBLE, NEW INTERNATIONAL VERSION®, NIV®, KING JAMES VERSION®, KJV®, NEW KING JAMES®, NKJV®
All rights reserved
Printed in USA

Book Review

Sharing testimonies is one of the ways that the Holy Spirit uses to keep us encouraged in the journey of faith. If you want to be quietly inspired by ordinary, devoted followers of the Lord Jesus who live in trusting relationships with an extraordinary God, I would like to recommend **Conversations of Grace**: *Blessings, Faith, Miracles & Courage*. This book is a collection of testimonies. Some tell the stories of special encounters and others testify to the gracious working of God in lifelong journeys experienced by members of the Bramalea Free Methodist Church.

I was especially intrigued by the way the initials of the congregation (BFMC) were reworked to also be an inspirational code: ***B**lessings,* ***F**aith,* ***M**iracles and* ***C**ourage* that the contributors to this book have adopted personally and have brought as a theme into the chapters that they have submitted. I started reading this little book on a day when I was stressed and a bit discouraged. By the time I had finished it, the Holy Spirit had used it to lift my spirits and to adjust my perspectives.

Rev. Keith Elford
Bishop, Free Methodist Church in Canada

Table of Contents

Acknowledgements 08
Foreword 10
Pastor's Message 11
Introduction 12
Our Testimonies 15
- What Jesus Means to Me by BFMC's Kingdom Kids............. 17
- Perseverance by David Reed 20
- Following in my Sister's Footstep by Joanne Belgrave 25
- Forgiveness – A Blessing from God by Ovid Wilson 26
- Touch Not the Lord's Anointed by Daisy Wright 30
- Survival Through God's Eyes by Frances Ebun Wright 33
- Waiting on God by Lynn and Henry Dyck 35
- My Journey With my Granddaughter by Maglyn Rose.......... 37
- The Garden at Bramalea by David Wright 39
- The Evolution of Spirit by Elsa Kelly................................... 43
- Giving God Thanks and Praise by Mella J. Rose.................... 47
- Prayer is the Key and Faith Unlocks the Door
  by Marcia Wright.. 50
- When God Answered by Daisy Wright................................. 52
- Letting Go of Anger and Fear - Anonymous......................... 54
- Through the Valley by June Rock... 56
- Qualities of a Good Lay Person by Rev. Keith E. Lohnes......... 62
- You are Never Alone by Caroline Haynes 64
- God's Awesome Love by Isaac Burnett 66
- God Opens Doors by Ida Chatham 69
- This is my Story by Ronjel Elaine Stuart............................... 70
- When God is Near by Unita Sam-Darling 76
- The Longer our Battle by Monique Peynado 78
- My Blessings, Faith, Miracles and Courage by Sister V 80

- Reflections of Faith, Love and Friendship
  by Trevor Hitchman……………………………………….. 84
- Faith Roots: An Enlightening Discovery by Esther Sarpong ….. 87
- How a Woman's League Led me to Christ by Ida Chatham…… 94
- Fix Your Eyes on Jesus by Christa Ball……………………………. 95
- Raising Awareness About Sickle Cell Disease by Louis Isaacs….. 97
- Special Words in a Successful Marriage
  by Rev. Keith E. Lohnes……………………………………… 100
- Tribute to Gran by Bri-Anne Smith……………………………. 102
- A Personal Relationship with Christ – Anonymous ………….. 107
- Train Up a Child in the Way of the Lord
  by George W. B. Edwards……………………………………. 111
- A Prayer and Praise to my Heavenly Father
  by Edith H. Edwards …………………………………………. 115
- An Amazing Discovery by E. Gael Lohnes ….………………… 117
- The Day I Lost my Faith by D. Monica Johnson……………….. 118

Spiritual Expressions in Poetry, Prose and Verse…………………. 121
- The ABCs of the Bible by Yimika……………………………. 123
- It Wasn't Much to Look at by Sue Caldwell-Reed……………… 127
- The Almighty God is Sufficient for Me by Yimika…………….. 129
- Creativity by Unita Sam-Darling……………………………. 131
- God's Love by Unita Sam-Darling……………………………. 133
- Learn to Depend on the Lord by Iris Chang……………………. 134
- What BFMC Means by Daisy Wright & June Rock……………... 135

Our Church……...……………………………………………. 139
- BFMC – From Humble Beginnings………………………………. 141
- BFMC – A Community of Diverse People by Yimika…..……... 143
- Many Hands and Hearts Join in Fellowship by Louis Isaacs…. 146
- Leading by Grace by Audrey Isaacs & Jackie Piper……………. 149
- Connections Team by Joanne P. Belgrave……………………. 151
- Keeping God's House Safe and Secure by Sam Boison………... 152

- Women Active in Service by Judith Sylvestre, Helen Charles & Edna Lawes 153
- Making a Joyful Noise Unto the Lord by Dave Reed................ 157

Spiritual Knowledge Builders.. 159
- Bible Word Search by Isaac Burnett..................................... 161
- Biblical Anagrams 1 by Isaac Burnett.................................. 162
- Bible Trivia by Isaac Burnett.. 163
- Bible Crossword Puzzle by Yimika....................................... 165
- Biblical Anagrams 2 by Isaac Burnett.................................. 167

References.. 168

List of Contributors 169

Acknowledgements

Conversations of Grace is a collection of stories written from the heart by members and friends of Bramalea Free Methodist Church in Brampton, Ontario. The book is God-centred and depicts a loving and merciful Father who hears the petitions and supplications of His children, and who answers prayers when we diligently seek Him and put our trust in Him.

Stories tell of overcoming adversities of various kinds and celebrating the joys and peace, which only He can give. We are moved by the authentic nature in which the stories are told. By sharing these personal experiences with others, the writers have demonstrated their unwavering hope in God through Jesus Christ our Lord. It is our hope that their stories will resonate with the readers who will be inspired, strengthened and blessed in whatever circumstance of life they may be.

We acknowledge and sincerely thank all the contributors, young and old, for letting us into their hearts and minds through their stories. From the simple words of faith and what God means to the kids, to the intense, soul-searching narratives of others, we find the true expressions of God working in our lives and shaping us as we seek first His kingdom and its righteousness.

Our special thanks go to Sister Veronica Crick whose concept of the initials of BFMC provided us an acronym: **B** for **Blessings, F** for **Faith, M** for **Miracles** and **C** for **Courage**. We are grateful to Rev. Keith E. Lohnes for writing the foreword and to Pastor

Dennis Ball for his message. We are indebted to the governing Board for its financial support in seeing us through with this project.

We would like to thank Bishop Keith Elford who wrote the first review of the book.

We also express our thanks to the Big, Bold, Book Idea team: Jasmine Rock who designed the book cover, Daisy Wright for her leadership, and Isaac Burnett, June Rock and David Wright for their untiring effort in making this book a reality.

We extend our appreciation to the editor Angela Carter and the designers Hemant and Mona Lal for their professional work in producing this book of such high quality and value. To all those who in diverse ways, through prayers, encouragement, lending a listening ear or a helping hand, we say sincere thanks and may God richly bless you all.

Foreword

Strength in Telling Our Story

By Rev. Keith E. Lohnes

Bramalea Free Methodist Church adopted the theme "Strength" as a focus for 2016. The Bible tells us that the joy of the Lord is our strength. (**Nehemiah 8:10**). When we have expressions of joy it often involves the telling of stories. Stories of God's redeeming work in individual lives make a compelling testimony for a watching world. As you read these stories, reflections and testimonies, rejoice with us that the story goes on and it speaks of the strength of the Lord revealed in individual lives. If the Lord is real in our lives, we all have a story to tell.

Jesus Christ was a master storyteller and through His stories and parables He revealed God's truth about redemption and daily living. Some of the Bible stories were about people of humble status, such as the widow who gave a tiny amount of money in the offering at the temple. She was honored for her sacrifice because it was all she had. And, now, almost 2,000 years later we read the story and are moved. The strength of that story has inspired believers for centuries to be generous in giving.

May the Lord bless these writings and use these expressions of His grace in people's lives to encourage all who read them.

We express our thanks to members of the editorial team, led by Daisy Wright, for their diligent work, as well as to all who contributed articles. May God receive all the glory.

Pastor's Message

The Power in Testimonies

By Pastor Dennis Ball

As I read the stories of all those who've submitted to this book, the verse that came to mind was Revelation 12:11, *"They have conquered him by the blood of the Lamb and by their testimony."* For me, this is what Conversations of Grace is all about. People telling their stories of how Jesus, the Lamb, conquered the sin in their lives by taking their sin upon Himself: Breaking the hold Satan had on their lives by rising from the grave; dismissing Satan's accusations against them by being seated at the right hand of the Father, and continually transforming them into the image of Christ by sending the Holy Spirit.

These stories remind me that we each have a story like this and they are more powerful than we realize. One person's testimony is more powerful than any sermon or any worship song can do to help guide, encourage or convict one another on this journey. Unfortunately, we sometimes give in to fear and withhold such blessings from others. So my prayer is that Conversations of Grace will inspire and encourage you to tell your story to those who He brings into your life.

Introduction

Gifts of Blessings, Faith, Miracles and Courage

And God has placed in the church first of all apostles, second prophets, third teachers, then miracles, then gifts of healing, of helping, of guidance, and of different kinds of tongues

1 Corinthians 12:28

"We need to tell our children and grandchildren about God... we need to tell our Christian stories to future generations...we need to reach people around the world...we don't know how our story will touch others," said Rev. Keith E. Lohnes in one of his sermons delivered in 2015.

Unknown to him, his message firmly established an idea that a member had been praying about and which she had previously discussed with the Board chair. She had suggested that the Bramalea Free Methodist Church (BFMC) family collectively write a book of stories about their Christian walk – stories that would encourage and inspire readers regardless of the trials they are facing. Hearing these words from Rev. Keith E. Lohnes that morning, she was overcome with the conviction that this was God's way of saying He approved.

This idea came at a time when lots of changes were taking place at BFMC. In 2014, our pastor, Rev. William "Rusty" Crozier, had just left, attendance was down and Sunday School had all but vanished. It would have been easy for the congregation to give up – but they didn't. The Board provided the leadership that the church needed and made the necessary pulpit arrangements to mitigate the disruption of not having a pastor. All the other ministries and teams – finance, hospitality, maintenance, women, men, worship and usher – continued their work.

BFMC was built on perseverance and had a long history of resilience. This determination was revealed during our time of struggle. In an organic way, people stepped up to use their gifts. One member had already assumed the leadership of the Men's Ministry. Another introduced the idea of a community vegetable garden, which was readily supported by the BFMC family. When an appeal went out for Sunday School teachers, many women – mainly grandmothers – volunteered to be a part of that ministry.

Another member who discovered a leaky faucet in one of the bathrooms, used his gift of plumbing to fix the problem. One member's husband (he does not attend BFMC), noticed that a part of the roof needed some minor repairs and did it. Yet another member decided that during 2016, she would bake birthday cakes for each Sunday School child. These are just a few of the many small acts being done by the congregation of BFMC without any fanfare.

It was while these struggles were taking place that the idea for the book was conceived. It was felt that instead of focusing on the struggles, people could contribute their personal stories of blessings, faith, miracles and courage to this book. It would also provide a way for some people to get involved in the life of BFMC. The "Big Bold Book Idea" became a reality and a committee of five was struck.

As stated earlier, the main aim of the book is to provide members with the opportunity to tell their stories in order to strengthen, encourage and inspire one another and, hopefully, bring people to Christ. It would also allow the Church family to live its mission: *"A diverse people moving with one mind in cheerful, humble obedience to further the Mission and Kingdom of God in Brampton and beyond."*

The name of the book, **Conversations of Grace**, is adopted from an aspect of our worship service during which people have short conversations with each other, exchange greetings and share prayer requests and happenings of the previous week. Another objective of this practice was for each person to deliberately seek out new faces and introduce these visitors to the congregation.

Conversations of Grace is a faith-based collection of writings and testimonies submitted by members and friends of BFMC. These testimonies demonstrate the presence and workings of God in the lives of each of its writers. By exploring these stories, readers can get a sense of God's grace in the lives of others. Several Sunday School children have also contributed to the book, giving short answers to the question "What Jesus means to me?"

In May 2016, BFMC celebrated its 34th anniversary. Over the years the church has accumulated a lot of history, which we are also sharing. So what started as a book of personal stories has expanded to include a short history of BFMC and the various roles within the Church. We at BFMC are encouraged by the potential of this book to bring about spiritual change in the lives of readers. It is our sincere wish that everyone who reads it will be blessed by these testimonies of Blessings, Faith, Miracles and Courage. We encourage you to own, relish, cherish and share a copy of **Conversations of Grace** with your families and friends.

OUR TESTIMONIES

What Jesus Means to Me

By BFMC's Kingdom Kids

Jesus called the children to him and said, "Let the little children come to me, and do not hinder them, for the kingdom of God belongs to such as these."

Luke 18:16

This section of the book is referred to as "Children's Moments", the segment of the worship service at BFMC when the children, fondly referred to as "Kingdom Kids", come forward to receive a short address and prayer from the Pastor before they are dismissed for Sunday School.

Sunday School at BFMC has had many teachers over the years, but we can truly state that all of our volunteers came equipped with a love for God, a love for children and a desire to teach our little ones to know God the Father, Son and Holy Spirit.

We introduce the Bible as the Christian's guide to living and aim to instill Christian principles such as being kind, loving and helpful. Our goal is to teach the children that Jesus will always be with them, that they can love God with all their hearts and that they can adhere to His Word every day with the help of the Holy Spirit.

For this book, the children were asked to say what Jesus means to them in a few words. Here are their impromptu answers:

Jazmine Rose-Brown (Age 7)
Jesus is love: He is my Saviour; He is my Guide; He is my Friend.

Dakari Medwinter (Age 8)
Jesus is Love…He loves me and He loves all of us.

(When Dakari was five years old, his mom's car got stuck in the snow while she was taking him to school. After they got going again, he turned to her and said: "Mom, when next you get stuck, ask Jesus for help".)

Francine Twmasi (Age 10)
Jesus is Love, Faith, Christ, Life, Gratefulness, Kindness, Son of God, Brave, Generous, Sacrifice and Healer.

Eriyana Powell (Age 11)
Jesus is: Life, a Hero and Saviour.

Cheyenne Meme (Age 4) and Jochebed Meme (Age 6)
Jesus is Love

Mirabel Meme (Age 8)
He gives me life. He is a nice person. He loves us.

Arianna Estridge (Age 8)
He is Love and Parents.

Jeremi Duncan (Age 7)
He gives me life. He saves my parents' lives. He died on the cross for me. He makes winter.

Jazmin Duncan (Age 5)
He gives me food. He is my Friend. He takes me to Chuck E Cheese.

Jocelyn Belgrave (Age 8) and Jaiden Belgrave (Age 10)
Jesus makes me feel happy, loved, hope, and we believe in Him.

Gabryel Wasmund (Age 6)
Jesus means to me to live, love others and be healthy.

Janelle Gritter (Age 3) and Micah Gritter (Age 6)
Jesus means love, joy, nice and good to me.

Quinton Louis (Age 8)
Jesus means love, kind, nice, joy and caring.

Courtney Louis (Age 6)
Jesus makes butterflies, dogs and babies.

Beth Zamora (Age 11)
Jesus means that we have to pray a lot and we love everyone.

Chrisna Zamora (Age 8)
Jesus means love. Jesus guides us. He made a lot of things in the world.

Naomi Rosa (Age 4)
He gives us food to eat.

Eva Rose (Age 8)
Jesus gives me a good family and He takes care of me.

Ross Sunglao (Age 11)
Jesus is my Friend, my Saviour and my heavenly Father. He loves me, watches me while I am asleep. He has done many miracles and one of them is "Me".

Perseverance

By Dave Reed

My wife Sue and I, along with daughter Danielle who was almost two, moved to Brampton to be closer to work opportunities. The population at that time was 123,814. We lived on Kennedy Road South, not far from Kennedy Road Tabernacle (KRT), a large and well known church at the time. We had moved from Belleville where we were involved in Centennial Free Methodist Church but there was not a local Free Methodist congregation in Brampton, so we occasionally attended KRT. Unknown to us, some years before this, area leaders of the Free Methodist Church in Canada had purchased a large piece of property in Brampton on Howden Boulevard. The District Superintendent, Rev. Earl S. Bull, father of Rev. Carl Bull (who later pastored BFMC), was one of the leaders involved in that process.

Sue and I also occasionally attended the nearest Free Methodist Church – Kingsview in Etobicoke. During this time, Rev. Bull continued to have an eye toward establishing a local Free Methodist society in Brampton and became aware that we were potential candidates to be involved in this endeavour. So, in the spring of 1980 (population 142,590), Rev. Bull contacted us about joining a Bible study that was starting in the area. The plan was to form the basis of a congregation that would someday occupy that site on Howden Boulevard.

Sue loves to remind me of that first Bible study – hosted at the home of Doug and Carolyn Gonyou on Grassington Crescent. I was unable to attend since I was very involved in a Gospel group and had rehearsal that evening. Since we now had a second child – daughter Darcy who was about 10 months old at the time – it was decided that I would take Danielle with me to rehearsal and Sue would take Darcy to the Bible study. Here's the scene: Doug and Carolyn; Carolyn's father, Bishop Donald N. Bastian; outgoing District Superintendent Rev. Bull; the newly installed incoming District Superintendent, Rev. Robert Buchanan, Sue and Darcy. Wow! All the Free Methodist heavyweights sat on one side of the room, facing Sue and Darcy on the other side. Sue figured they knew all the answers so it was all on her shoulders. No pressure!

And so it began.

As the Bible study grew to the point of needing more space, we moved to a new meeting place at Lester B. Pearson Catholic School. During this period, the congregation was established as a society of the Free Methodist Church on May 2, 1982 (population 160,766). Our first son, Jon-Paul was born that year (as was Emily Gonyou). Rev. Carl Bull used to have Jon-Paul and Emily come to the front of the church on anniversary Sunday as a visual reminder of how old we were as a congregation.

Sometime during 1982, we became aware that significant rental increases were coming at Lester B. Pearson, and in a very providential way, we were made aware of another option. At the time, the Peel Board of Education had a concept known as the Community School program. In exchange for taking some training on how to open and close the facility (alarm, clean up, etc.) and for being available to open and close the school for user groups periodically, the Church had use of the gym, chairs, a piano and the staff room on Sundays – for NO CHARGE! No charge is a big deal for Free Methodists (humour) so we were really excited and felt blessed that God had opened this door for us. By the way, the school building we used was Massey St. Public School – still going strong. As it happened, we lived five minutes from the school and all our kids attended there.

Naturally, we played our part in opening and closing as well as setting up and tearing down for each Sunday. Good times!

We continued to worship at Massey St. Public School and dreamed of a day when we would have our own church building. Our family continued to expand. In 1984 (population 178,343) our second son David Jr. was born. During this time the congregation grew as well, fuelled in part by the anticipation of, and planning for, our new church home. In 1989 (population 223,964) construction began at the Howden Boulevard site.

The process relied heavily on volunteer labour from among the congregation and was spearheaded by Ron Horne who was affectionately named "Volunteer Vern." Ron kept us informed and inspired as the project unfolded. In the end, Rev. Carl Bull logged the most volunteer hours of anyone, a distinction he wore with modesty and grace. For many of us, the most memorable service during that time was Christmas Eve 1989. The new building was not ready for occupancy for a few months yet, but had reached a stage that, with a portable salamander construction heater, a bunch of lawn chairs and the seats from our old Dodge van, we were able to hold an "authentic" candlelight service. Perhaps the most memorable Christmas Eve service I have ever been involved in! The building reached completion in 1990 and was dedicated in the fall of that year.

The following year, 1991 (population 242,660) our son Nathan was born. Sue reminded me that Nathan was dedicated on Christmas Eve of that year. Remember that thing I said about most memorable Christmas Eve? This may have trumped that – but you get the idea. I guess as time passes you forget about all the great stuff that has happened to you.

Not everything was great though. Sue's mom, Hester, passed away in 1993 and her funeral was at the church. Many of the hymnals and platform furnishings were dedicated in memory of Hester and her family. And then there was, for me, a defining moment in our lives as a family and as a church family. In July 1995 our first grandson Tyler was born to our daughter Darcy who was 16 at the time. The love and mercy that was extended toward Darcy (and us) demonstrated what I believe the Church should be. Tyler increased the population of Brampton by one (269,754).

Sue and I had one more addition to our family, Colin born in 1997 (population 289,140). As our older kids began to move on (for various reasons) Nathan and Colin became regulars in the sound booth, always ready (if not willing) to push the buttons. I must say here how much I have appreciated our children over the years. They humored us and truly helped us to fulfill what we felt we needed to do as members of BFMC. Much thanks to Sue who often had to carry on in my absence as I travelled with **Reunion** until I retired from the group in December 2012 (population about 525,000).

So, we have lived in Brampton for almost 38 years. Nearly all of those years we have been involved with BFMC, from the earliest beginnings up to the present. We have seen wonderful pastors and friends come and go. And yes – there have been ups and downs too.

The group of Christ followers we serve with at present (January 2016) are a treasure to us and a testament to the faithfulness of God to do his work in and through us. Our story as a congregation and our story as a family is still unfolding. In **Hebrews 11** the writer defines faith and talks about the giants of the faith from scripture, then in verse 13 writes: *"All these people were still living by faith when they died. They did not receive the things promised; they only saw them and welcomed them from a distance, admitting that they were foreigners and strangers on earth."*

Our Testimonies

Our new pastor, Dennis Ball, has encouraged each of us to choose a defining word for 2016. Mine is **PERSEVERANCE**. The thought that goes with that comes from **Hebrews 12:1-3**. This is from the *Message* translation:

> *Do you see what this means—all these pioneers who blazed the way, all these veterans cheering us on? It means we'd better get on with it. Strip down, start running—and never quit! No extra spiritual fat, no parasitic sins. Keep your eyes on Jesus, who both began and finished this race we're in. Study how he did it. Because he never lost sight of where he was headed—that exhilarating finish in and with God—he could put up with anything along the way: Cross, shame, whatever. And now he's there, in the place of honor, right alongside God. When you find yourselves flagging in your faith, go over that story again, item by item, that long litany of hostility he plowed through. That will shoot adrenaline into your souls!*

Following in my Sister's Footsteps

By Joanne P. Belgrave

The Lord will watch over your coming and going both now and forevermore.

Psalms 121:8

I was at home one Sunday around 8 a.m. The sun was just coming in through my window. So I decided to get out of the bed, stop feeling sorry for myself and get to church.

For years I was blaming God for all the things that happened in my life and the people who just walked away when I needed them. It was a bright, sunny morning in the summer of 1996 when I walked into Bramalea Free Methodist Church and was welcomed with open arms. I had people looking at me and saying welcome back, which was odd because I never met them before in my life. I did try to say I did not know you but got lots of hugs which softened my heart.

I've been at BFMC for over 19 years and I am grateful for the family I have here. I learned years after that my younger sister and her family were at the church before I was. (The hugs were meant for her but I needed them at that time).

That's the reason for my title.

God bless you and your family.

Forgiveness—A Blessing from God

By Ovid Wilson

In the Gospel of **Luke 6:7** we are called upon to "forgive and you shall be forgiven." It is my opinion that in some situations we are called upon not only to forgive but sometimes, as I would put it, offer the gift of forgiveness to others.

Many years ago, a family dispute arose between my father and his elder sister over property my grandfather had willed among his children. I would not go into the details, but I want to mention that my father was very lenient while on the other hand my aunt pursued the matter very aggressively to the point where the law courts became involved. Obviously this brought discord in the family, but my dad always admonished us to continue to be respectful to our elder family members involved in this bitter dispute. Sometimes I found it difficult to understand some of my father's actions but later in life as I matured, I came to realize that he was just practicing what Christ meant when He asks us to forgive.

I recall one incident which occurred while all of this feud was going on. One morning I was driving my father from the countryside where we lived to attend a court hearing in the city. As we were travelling through the village where my aunt, his sister, lived, I saw her standing by the roadside waiting for transportation to go to the city to appear in the same court he was going to. Put yourself in my position. Honestly, I did not know what to do – whether to drive past her or stop and offer her a ride. My dad made that decision for me, a decision which had me baffled but not surprised because she was the one who had taken this dispute to the court. He told me to stop the car and offer her a ride. I had passed her a few feet by this time, so I backed up and he opened the back door and invited her in. She blatantly refused and, despite his pleadings, even to the point of telling her she did not have to say anything to him if she didn't want to, she did not budge, so we continued on our way.

My cousin, my aunt's oldest daughter, reacted similarly to this whole situation. She stopped speaking to me. We would be approaching each other on the same street but she would walk past me as though I were a complete stranger. After I emigrated to Canada I would still inquire occasionally from other family members about her. She subsequently emigrated to the USA and I was devastated to learn that she had been diagnosed with an incurable disease.

Before I left for Canada, my father went home to be with the Lord and he and his sister never reconciled. She attended his funeral and, even though it was 33 years ago, I can practically hear her shrill voice shouting at the end of the funeral service, "Oh God, my brother. Look what you have done to me! You have gone your way and I did not get the opportunity to tell you I was sorry and to ask for your forgiveness."

If you have a reason to forgive someone or to ask for someone's forgiveness, do it now. Do not wait for tomorrow, next week, next month, next year or, as some would say, "When I am good and ready," because chances are that tomorrow may never come.

I did not want history to repeat itself. There was no way to communicate with my cousin since she had isolated herself from the family, but I thought about it and prayed for her and for an opportunity to get in contact with her. God is good and God answers prayers and through his grace he provided that opportunity for me.

My other cousin, who is another aunt's daughter residing in Baltimore, USA, was getting married and I received an invitation to the wedding. These two cousins were very close and I found out that the one who I could not reach would be at the wedding and I resolved to take full advantage of this opportunity.

Ironically, the Saturday of the weekend before the wedding I attended Men's Bible Fellowship at my church, BFMC. The topic for that day was about forgiveness and during our discussion I shared my situation with the group. The passage of Scripture found in **Matthew 18:15-17** was brought to our attention and discussed at length. I left that meeting more convinced that God was placing it upon me to take the initiative to resolve this matter.

Early the following Friday morning, accompanied by two of my brothers, we left for the long drive to the USA to attend the wedding. We arrived there in the afternoon in time for the wedding rehearsal and dinner afterwards. We then proceeded to the hotel where all the other family members were staying. My cousin was not at the rehearsal, but I was told that she was at the hotel. In the hotel lobby, I met another relative who told me which floor the family was occupying.

God moves in mysterious ways, his wonders to perform. I approached the elevators and pressed the button and waited for a short while for an elevator to come. When the elevator came and the door slid open, there was one passenger on board and, to my surprise, it was my cousin who I wanted to see. With open arms, I rushed into the elevator without even thinking how she would react. I hugged her and told her how happy I was to see her. As she hugged me back I saw the tears rolling down her cheeks and I knew that those were tears of relief, knowing that I had chosen to forgive her even though she did not ask. We talked and talked at length, not once mentioning what had happened in the past.

We had an enjoyable evening at the wedding and on the Sunday morning we sat together at the family brunch and talked more until we all had to leave for our different destinations. Sad to say, that was the last conversation I had with her as her condition worsened and she went home to be with the Lord.

I attended her funeral and, at the conclusion of the service, we were singing the closing hymn, **God Be with You till we Meet Again.** We reached the end of the first verse and the congregation stopped singing because the chorus, *"Till we meet, till we meet, till we meet at Jesus' feet. Till we meet, till we meet. God be with you till we meet again"* was omitted from the song sheet.

There was much discord when they tried to sing the next verse. The service moderator asked the officiating pastor if he could continue leading the hymn but he said he did not know it. He asked the musician to play it, but he did not know the hymn either.

As the pastor was about to pronounce the benediction, I raised my hand and the pastor said, "Brother, do you know the song?" "Yes," I replied, and then proceeded to the podium and led the congregation in singing the hymn in its entirety. At the end of the hymn, I repeated the refrain and when I was done, I walked over to the casket, knelt on a stool beside it and quietly whispered, "Rest in peace 'til we meet again."

I left the funeral service knowing that she was at peace and happy to know that I had given her the opportunity to experience forgiveness by obeying what God had called me to do.

Touch Not the Lord's Anointed

By Daisy Wright

Do not touch my anointed ones; do my prophets no harm.
Psalm 105:15; 1 Chronicles 16:22

The message of this story is to remind you, dear reader, that when you give God your concerns, you are to leave them with Him. He can handle it all.

My daughter was involved in an accident in 2006. She arrived at an intersection when the traffic light was turning amber. A motorist entering the same intersection from the opposite direction made a left turn and slammed into my daughter's car. While my daughter was still trapped in the car, the woman had already hopped out of her vehicle, got to my daughter and, with flailing arms, began swearing at her.

The police were called and although one eyewitness told him the light was on amber when my daughter was going through, he still issued her a ticket. She contested it in court, and it was thrown out.

Almost two years afterwards, one week before the statute of limitations had passed, I heard a knock on my door. The courier gave me two letters – one with my name on it. I opened the letter and gasped. The woman was suing both my daughter and me for a host of things. I was in shock and the only thing that came to mind was to hold the letter up to the ceiling and cry out: "Touch not the Lord's anointed." How those words came to my mouth is still a mystery to me.

I telephoned my husband who advised me to inform the insurance company. Several years went by and my daughter received a letter from a lawyer for the insurance company. The lawyer wanted to meet with her to see if they should settle the case. I accompanied my daughter to the meeting but was not allowed in. Prior to that, the lawyer asked my daughter to relate what she remembered of the event. She gave the details: yes, the police were called; no, an ambulance was not present. She explained that even before she was able to get out of the vehicle the woman had come over to her vehicle swearing and talking about her pending wedding in two weeks.

My daughter and the lawyer went into the meeting and when it was over, the lawyer congratulated my daughter on presenting her side of the story. She then said, "And, we will not be settling the case."

Another two years passed. On Friday, September 13, 2013, I woke up from a dream. I dreamt that my mom was at a podium in a wide-brimmed black hat speaking. Other than my mom, the only person I recognized in the audience was one of my aunts. My mom was speaking with much vigour and the only sentence I remembered hearing was, "Don't I tell you when you give God things you should leave it and keep it there?" I said to myself, "If my mom and big sister were alive, I would've called them to tell them of the dream, because those were the exact words my mom frequently said to us. I would tell her of things I was praying about, while simultaneously trying to handle the situation by myself, and she would tell me once I turned it over to God I should let it go.

So, my dream was on September 13, 2013. The following Wednesday, September 18, my daughter had picked up the mail and as she came through the door, she called out and said, "Mom, they threw out the case!" I asked her what case, thinking it was related to a very hot issue that was happening in the US at the same time; that is, the case of Trayvon Martin, the young black man who was killed by a security guard in Florida. She said, "The insurance case! This is the letter from the court."

I ran downstairs and said to her, "Do you remember I told you how the day I received the letters from the woman's lawyer informing us that you and I were being sued, how I held up my letter and said 'touch not the Lord's anointed'?" She said she remembered. I then reminded her of what my mom had said in the dream.

We examined the chronology of events and how my dream tied in with the judge's decision, which was made on September 11, 2013. Two days later, on September 13, I had the dream about my mom. I concluded that my mom knew what the judge's ruling was and came to tell me in the dream. In fact, she came to remind me that when I give God my problems, I should leave them with Him. I should not take it upon myself to solve my problems.

What a revelation! My dear Mama was still giving me godly advice from beyond the grave. I share this story, not only because of the gift of a wonderful mother, but that you, dear reader, can believe that God is in charge, no matter your circumstances. Just leave all your problems in His care; do not take them back from Him. He is able, more than able!

Dear Lord,

Thank you for the gift of mothers, especially those who follow Your teachings. Their lives exemplify what it means to trust You. Help us to emulate their prayer life so that we, too, can put our trust in You. In Jesus' Name. Amen.

Survival Through God's Eyes

By Frances Ebun Wright

What is it you see when you look at me?

Do you see me for who I am or is your perception colored by decades of some stereotype?

If you met me on the street would you smile a welcoming smile or turn away and cross over to the other side with a tighter grip on your bag?

What do I see when I look at you? Do I think you are smarter by design or default, just because you wear glasses propped up on your nose? Do I think you are braver because you talk the loudest or that you are weaker because you don't say a word?

We are made in the image of God and are created equal in His sight.

He made us beautiful, you and I. You with your alabaster complexion, with hues from snow white to bronze, to all shades of brown from caramel to blue black. You with your beautiful eyes, big and round, or almond eyes ranging in size with colours of blue, green, brown and everything in between.

You with hair from bone straight to tightly curled, all of different textures, all glorious. And you with your full lips, your slender or broad nose, your slight frame or your curvy shape. All of us are fearfully and wonderfully made (**Psalm 139:14**).

Do I see your kind heart, your giving hand, your compassion and brilliance or have I not taken the time to marvel at God's awesome creation? Do I assume the worst to keep myself from hurt?

In trusting God, I am learning to give of myself fully and without reserve. Let's get to know each other, you and I. I promise not to prejudge you before I say hello. I promise to give you a chance to show me who you are and to believe you when you do. There are no mistakes in opening myself up to getting to know you. For at my most vulnerable, I am strong (**1Corinthians 12:10**) with the love of God in my heart. Where I am hurt, He will heal; when I am tempted, He will deliver, for He will not bring me more than I can bear (**1Corinthians 10:13**). Where I am loved, I will give thanks for there is no greater gift.

I am learning that to survive in this world, I have to continuously evaluate my heart's condition. Am I developing a hard heart or am I filled with the peace of God which transcends all understanding (**Philippians 4:7**). Am I easily offended or am I quick to forgive? The peaceable spirit, one that does not hold on to the past, one that seeks enlightenment and is more focused on giving more than receiving, is the one that will survive.

Waiting on God

By Lynn and Henry Dyck

God asks us to trust Him and to be patient while we wait for Him to work in our lives and the lives of those we love. His Word tells us in **1 Timothy 2:4** that God "wants all men to be saved and to come to a knowledge of the truth".

These are the truths which encouraged me (Lynn) for over 30 years as I prayed for my mother to give her heart to the Lord. I was raised in a home where Christian values were taught but my parents never went to church themselves. I was dropped off at Sunday School and became involved in weekly activities which nourished my love for the Lord, and eventually led me to a saving knowledge of Jesus and a confession of faith in Him.

My parents always supported me in these activities but never showed an interest in knowing God for themselves. My mom even went as far as holding up her hand to stop my husband and me when we tried to share Jesus with her. I prayed for my mom every day and so often I wondered why God didn't answer my prayers. Even so, I never gave up.

My father died in 1999. Shortly after, while visiting our church, my mom was challenged by one of our dear friends about her faith. The Holy Spirit was at work! Something our friend said spoke to my mom and, at the age of 72, she accepted Christ as her Saviour and Lord. Mom was baptized in her own church and I had the privilege of being present and being able to share my life verse with her: **Philippians 4:13**, *"I can do all things through Christ who strengthens me."*

Mom died three years after and on her death bed some of her last words to us were that she could hardly wait to go home and be with her Lord. She truly experienced the love and generous grace of God in her last few years. What an answer to prayer!

I've often been able to tell my story about my mom to encourage others who pray for loved ones and wonder if their prayers will ever be answered. God <u>does</u> hear our prayers and honours them in His own perfect time. We can always trust Him and always rely on Him. It's such a comfort for me to know that one day I will be reunited with my mom and dad in heaven where we will live together for eternity.

He is faithful. Always!

My Journey With my Granddaughter
Jazmine Rose-Brown

By Maglyn Rose

On April 13, 2010, a precious little girl came into the world and into my life. In spite of the pain and discomfort my daughter was going through at birth, I simply took the little one in my arms, and said, "To God be the glory, great things He has done" (Crosby, 1875).

From day one I presented her to the Lord. I have had bad days but the good days are too much to mention. As the days unfurled and the nights passed, this little baby got closer and closer to my heart. Her smile is enough to keep me throughout the day. I love this little girl without question.

I never thought of this day, that so early in her life she would be gone for an entire day. October 18, 2010, at six months five days, she started daycare. That day I will never forget as long as I live. My heart was broken in many pieces. I just couldn't leave her. I stayed and cried my eyes out. I got the assurance from the teachers that she would be safe so I finally walked away, but in my journey on the bus home I felt pain. I had to question myself "why" but I prayed and prayed, asking God to keep watch over her, the rest of the kids and their teachers; to build a fence around them, and dispatch an angel from heaven to keep watch. I know he heard my cry. She became the apple of their eyes and was affectionately called "Centre Piece." She was loved by everyone.

Jasmine grew up in BFMC. She was blessed there and became known to all the members, loved and cared for by all. On many,

many occasions she would be the only child present. I taught her to love the Lord, to pray and trust him. She is now able to stand up, repeat the Lord's Prayer and recite the Bible verse **John 3:16:** "For God so loved the world…"

She loves to be at church. Unfortunately, at one point there wasn't any Sunday School and she was sad. Finally, an announcement was made that Sunday School would begin again. She hugged me and said Grandma, "My dreams have come true." She was so happy. This little girl is a shining light. I pray she will continue in this path.

Dear Lord,

I thank you for everything and for blessing us all with this precious little girl. Please help me to continue praying for her. To God be the glory, great things He always does.

The Garden at Bramalea

By David Wright

Several years ago, a former youth member, Ethan Horne, decided that he wanted to start a vegetable garden at our church and donate the proceeds to a local food bank. He and his Dad, Ron, faithfully tended the garden and the fruits and vegetables of their labour were donated to Ste. Louise Outreach Centre of Peel. This was a demonstration of **Isaiah 11:6** "…and a little child shall lead them."

Years passed and in early spring 2015, our members were invited again to collectively start a community vegetable garden on the same piece of church property.

The objectives of doing the garden were twofold: first, to engender a relational spirit of cooperation among members and promote a sense of community and connection with the environment; second, to manage and maintain the plot of land, put it into productive use and to grow fresh produce and plants that would be distributed to the community and to members of BFMC.

Fifteen volunteers signed up and $1,500 was generously donated for the purchase of triple mix soil, garden tools and seedlings and for tilling and preparing the soil. Our theme was "Happy gardening – Get involved and let's make BFMC'S community garden a showpiece of a faith-led, healthy church for healthy living and spiritual well-being."

With the wintery weather fading away rather hesitantly, the team of enthusiastic gardeners with skills and experience ranging from fair to excellent, set out on a balmy Saturday morning to arrange the beds and to plant the seedlings. They were informed about matters such as garden setup and upkeep; gardening procedures including watering, pruning, pest/disease control, harvesting and trash removal; ensuring that the garden was weeded and properly maintained, and, finally, the fall clean-up.

So what are the benefits of a community vegetable garden, some might ask? According to the City of Brampton's website, community gardens are beneficial because they improve health, personal wellbeing, community development and environmental stewardship; provide access to nutritionally rich foods and promote healthy eating; promote positive social interactions and increase a sense of wellness and belonging; promote inter-generational and cross-cultural connections; increase a sense of community ownership and stewardship; promote exposure to green space and outdoor physical activity; relieve stress, and improve mental health.

So, how do we relate our gardening experience to Biblical accounts? What were the lessons learned? How do we apply these lessons to our everyday lives and our interpersonal relations with those we come across at church, at home and in the community in general? We are reminded in the familiar hymn "We plough the field and scatter…" that we plow the field and plant the good seedling on the land, but it is fed and watered by God's almighty hand.

Like the parable of the sower and the seeds **(Luke 8:4-15)**, some of the seedlings were trampled on the paths, others eaten by bugs, and others, still, choked by weeds. Some, however, fell on fertile soil and yielded a bountiful harvest of tasty, organic tomatoes, peppers, callaloo, broccoli, collard greens, kale, peas/beans, herbs/spices, okra, squash and zucchini. Zucchini bread was a healthy delicacy and many people liked it.

Life's lesson: We should prepare our hearts as fertile ground for the seed, which is the Word of God, to grow in our hearts and to be a benefit to others and to ourselves. Otherwise, we may get lost in the myriad of life's trials and tribulations, and we don't become fruitful.

And, talking about weeds, the team worked tirelessly to uproot weeds that became a nuisance and competed with the plants for nutrients and water. What was striking was that we encountered a situation which, had it been in a church setting, may have baffled even the most discerning and seasoned pastor. Looking tender and similar to what we thought was squash, we let a particular plant grow in four places until it turned out to be nothing but a harmful bush with a voracious appetite, spreading its branches and suppressing the nearby plants – wolf in sheep's clothing, I thought.

Life's lesson: At harvest time as in the parable about the separation of the wheat and tares **(Matthew 13:24-30)** the weeds were separated from the vegetables and cast away. We are never to allow evil in all its various forms to dig deep roots into our lives, our homes, our church or anywhere else, or it would eventually overwhelm and devour us. We should discard every evil that turns us away from God, be faithful and pray, hope and trust that God will deliver us from the evil one. And as His children we must serve Him with all our heart, soul, mind and strength.

We were delighted at the good harvest. However, just as in **Matthew 9: 35-38**, the harvest was plentiful, but strangely, the workers were few. What a disappointment, we wondered! Members had the opportunity to pick fresh produce in return for small donations but some decided not to. Those who did recounted their pleasant experience of savouring freshly-picked veggies right at our doorsteps.

Life's lesson: We cannot afford to take a back seat in God's vineyard. We should be prepared to go into the world, our community, to spread the good news of Jesus Christ, His redeeming love and His sacrifice on the Cross of Calvary and resurrection to bring us eternal life. Using our God-given gifts and talents in furthering the mission and vision of BFMC requires commitment and service.

In conclusion, we knew it was going to be much fun, sweat and laughter, and so it was! Members devoted their time and energy to make sure that all went well, and interacted with each other on a friendly, cooperative basis. We watched the tiny seedlings grow into healthy plants, and it was a learning experience for many. At harvest time, we dedicated a bowl of choice vegetables at the altar and the pastor thanked God for His bountiful goodness and blessed our efforts.

Two baskets of vegetables were donated to two charitable organizations in Brampton as a goodwill gesture. With the end of the growing season, it was time for us to coordinate the fall clean-up and wrap up for the year. The dedication and devotion of all team members helped us to achieve our objectives successfully and we owe all our accomplishments to the grace and mercy of God to whom be all glory, power and praise.

The Evolution of Spirit

By Elsa Kelly

A **time to let go, a time to let God**

We recognize that ideas are all around us to be fully expressed. In that knowledge and awareness feel God's presence to support and encourage us all in launching these ideas into productive actions for the benefit of humanity. In building these ideas into their full expression, let go of fear, unworthiness and doubt and give way to courage, love, purpose, creativity and best intentions to bring these gifts to the world.

In time of need and clarity always remember that the door to unlocking the solution is right in front of you. And the key…prayer.

The Power of Deciding

The clutter of life traps so many of us into holding onto people and situations that are no longer serving or adding energy to our lives. Release yourself from these various forms of shackles and trust your heart to explore the path that leads you to becoming the best version of yourself.

At those critical life's crossroads, it all comes down to one key action…deciding. Deciding to be brave and courageous. Deciding to live and flourish versus simply existing, and walk on the path less traveled with God's love. Own your decision fully versus defaulting to blaming when the path gets a little rocky. If the path was easy everyone would be traveling on it. When you decide to choose the path that calls you to love yourself first, love yourself wholly and love yourself so that your "cup runneth over" and the love you can share with others is ever-flowing.

Become part of the growing and collective consciousness that decide to choose love and courage over fear and complacency. In choosing this path your cup will run over with love to share abundantly with others and keep yourself whole and complete to live your purpose.

Allow prayer and meditation to be your superfoods that nourish and maintain the strong faith required to persevere through even the most challenging and difficult times. In those vulnerable moments of self-doubt, pain and uncertainty, hold a special space in your heart for faith. Faith is the light that shines brightly in the direction that you are going so protect it and keep the flame going bright and strong especially in the darkest of hours. It will serve you well.

Gratitude and Spirit

Spirit is breath and breath is the ultimate necessity of life. It is with our first breath that spirit enters our body to fulfill its purpose in human form and in our last breath spirit leaves us in the same way. While here on the planet, protect and nourish your spirit by surrounding yourself with people who support you in fully shining your light so they too may be inspired and called to action. Insecurity, envy, jealousy and pettiness have no place for spirit to thrive and contribute to humanity. Remove the roadblocks in your life that aim to keep your spirit down and pigeon-holed. We've all heard of the "crab in the bucket" mentality and may have experienced the effect directly, indirectly or was the crab in someone's life.

The energy that is required to escape the crab and the energy the crab expends to keep people down is energetically draining for all involved. What is the quickest way for your spirit to move from energy-draining actions to energy-gaining actions? …Gratitude. So simple, so brilliantly powerful.

Rebuild your spirit and hold space in your heart on a daily basis for gratitude. Especially in those times when things just seem to be going sideways when you want to go straight, hold space for gratitude and experience God's love and support. It will add positive energy to encourage you on your path. Gratitude is not a fair-weather friend, gratitude is your friend in need and your spiritual cheerleader. In the same way breath is the ultimate necessity of life for us, gratitude is essential for spirit to thrive.

What a beautiful journey…the continuous journey of becoming. No matter the challenges, the process of becoming is simply life-altering. With that said, who are you "choosing" to become? Hold your power to become the greatest version of yourself and watch God open the doors and clear the path for you to do so. Living your truth is the ultimate gift you can give to yourself and to humanity.

Living a Joy-Filled Life

There's a saying that comes to mind when choosing to live in one's truth…believe in yourself, trust the process, change forever. With these powerful words comes the wonderful element of joy into the equation. Many would agree that life is not easy. With that said, how we choose to deal with life's curve balls and blind-sides is what makes it so exciting, rewarding and gratitude-filled. Joy allows us to remain present during precious moments with family and friends, embrace key life lessons along the way instead of keeping the focus solely on "getting there".

Love, laugh and embrace the adventures that this beautiful life has to offer. The simple acts of creating joy for others as we go about our daily lives can have an enormously positive impact in people's lives. The simple act of a smile, a hug, opening up the door for someone, calling someone out of the blue to say "hi." These seemingly tiny acts can bring immense joy to people who may be silently dealing with a difficult life situation. It's so easy to do, cost nothing yet is priceless in so many ways as we live in the joy to pay it forward.

Giving God Thanks and Praise

By Mella J. Rose

Thanks, thanks, I give you thanks
For all you've done.
I am so blessed, my soul is at rest
Oh Lord I give you thanks.

— **Carroll McGruder (1986)**

Giving God thanks and praise is sometimes what some people don't often do. Offering our praises and thanks to God is what He would want us to do.

I have so much to give God thanks for that I don't know where to start. I will converse as much as I can so you will have an idea where I am coming from. My Savior has done great things in my life and I can say that I am truly blessed. He paid the ultimate price for my sins. He suffered and died on the cross to redeem me. How can I repay Him for this? So, therefore, it gives me joy in sharing my journey with others and the hope that their lives will be impacted by this.

As a child growing up in the Caribbean, the church played a very important role in my life. I was blessed to have wonderful, caring, loving Christian parents – Lloyd and Sarah McDonald – who inspired my siblings and me and have established a solid foundation built on Christ Jesus' love for us to follow, which serves as a daily reminder for us.

Our parents always assured us that all things are possible only through Christ, if we only believe and trust in Him. Emphasis was placed on us to always give Him praise and thanks for what He has done for us no matter how small. To continue this, we reserved special time in our home to spend with the Lord. For example, every day my siblings and I would get up early in the morning at 5 o'clock. That's when our daily devotion would begin. Our parents would say, "We need God's guidance to be with us during the day." Also, it gave us time to talk with God.

When I reflect on those days, that was an early time of the day to be up for devotions but somehow we didn't frown because deep down we knew that it was good for us and the right thing to do. I can truly say we were committed and very disciplined. What better way to start off your day than with Jesus by your side! That kept us grounded. It also reminded us that without God in our lives, there would be no progress.

The progression of our thanks and praises continued as we attended church and Sunday School. This is where we interacted with other children and learned more about God. I enjoyed Sunday School because this was where I personally learned to read the Bible the most, the teachings and of God's love for everyone.

Our Sunday School teacher was Ms. Fulford, a Peace Corps worker from England. She was someone truly sent from God to us at Alderton Methodist Church in my small town. She was instrumental in helping us read and understand the Bible. She took pains as she emphasized Jesus as being the centre of our lives, which we understood well. The many songs we learned about Jesus and His love for us are deeply rooted in my memory.

As I looked back over the past years, there were many instances that I can recall for which to give God thanks and praise. God directed my path when I emigrated to Canada in the late 60s.

God has blessed me with a good life and for that I am so very thankful.

God has blessed me with a wonderful family. My husband Noel is my childhood sweetheart and of the same belief as mine in Jesus Christ. We have three grown children – Michael, Diane and Dwayne – and God has blessed them with families of their own. I have instilled in my children and grandchildren the love of God and I have faith that the good Lord will bring them closer to Him someday soon.

I have learned much in my life through the grace of God. And I will continue to give Him thanks and praise. I gave my life over to Him and have not looked back. I found peace in God as I walk in His light. This light radiates as I get older. I have found a church I can call home at Bramalea Free Methodist Church where the word of God is being preached, where people are of one accord and dwell in Jesus Christ.

God has a plan for all of us. Let us then continue to give Him the praise and thanks He deserves. And this can only be accomplished if we believe and trust in Him.

Thanks for those who have set the examples and the teaching of His words to me.

Most of all I thank my parents, Sunday School teachers and others who have set the foundation that helped me to see the light of Jesus. This will remain in me forever.

Prayer is the Key, and Faith Unlocks the Door

By Marcia Wright

Since my early childhood I went to Sunday school with my parents, grandparents, aunts, uncles and siblings. Sundays were worship days and also family days – extremely happy days. As a child I was enrolled in Cradle Roll Certification (birthday celebration). As the years went by, Sunday School exams were introduced. I participated in summer school, summer camp, young people's group and the Women's League within the Beechamville Methodist Church in Jamaica.

In the Jamaica District of Methodist Churches there are a number of circuits and I was a part of the Beechamville and Bensonton Circuit, which is located in the parish of St. Ann, Jamaica. The first Sunday of January is celebrated as Covenant Sunday. Harvest/Thanksgiving is celebrated in the month of February and March/April is Easter, both of which are major celebrations. John Wesley or Aldersgate Day is celebrated in May. On this day, all 13 churches gather at one location for a service of praise, worship and banner competition, which depicts the theme for that particular year. September is the month for Missions and, of course, Christmas in December. The week before Christmas I would participate in caroling in the wee hours of the morning.

Teen years were a bit more difficult and my interest changed but the foundation was still there. By my 20s I realized something was missing from my life and so I decided to follow Jesus. After emigrating to Canada I found Bramalea Free Methodist Church and to date I am still worshipping with the congregation. I have taught my two children to love and serve the Lord.

Along the way there have been trials and tribulations, but with each one I prayed and with God's help I have overcome. For me, I start and end each day with prayer. While walking through an airport gift shop on one of my vacations to Jamaica I purchased a keychain which depicts the map of Jamaica with these words inscribed: "Prayer is the key, Faith unlocks the door." This has been a constant reminder for me every day that "prayer is the key."

When God Answered

By Daisy Wright

*For I know the plans I have for you, declares the L*ORD*, plans to prosper you and not to harm you, plans to give you hope and a future.*

Jeremiah 29:11

I had just finished praying and got into bed. As I was lying there I asked God a question. I said, "God, I know you have answered my small prayers but when are you going to answer some of the big ones?"

With the question on my mind I fell asleep. During my sleep I dreamt that I saw this huge billboard on a highway, looking like a blackboard in a classroom. On the board, written in chalk, was **Jeremiah 29:11**. It was not the full text of the verse – just the reference. I knew exactly what it said, because it's one of my favourite verses of the Bible. The following morning, I opened my Bible to the passage:

*"For I know the plans I have for you," declares the L*ORD*, "plans to prosper you and not to harm you, plans to give you hope and a future."*

I became very quiet. I thought about the question I had asked God the night before, and how his answer came swiftly. It wasn't the answer to my big prayer as I had asked, but it was the answer He thought fit to give me. He pointed me to the verse as a reminder that He knows the plans he has for me, so I shouldn't worry.

I have pondered on that verse many times since and whenever I am venturing on a new project, I always place it in the Lord's hand because I know, without a doubt, that He has plans for me.

Have you ever asked God why he isn't answering your prayers? Stay in faith. He is answering them right now. As my mom always said, "God answers every prayer: It's either 'yes', 'no' or 'wait'."

Letting Go of Anger and Fear

Anonymous

Almost ten years ago, life took an unexpected turn. I was forever changed, both in my faith and outlook. It made sure that I learned both to see and appreciate the ways God makes even bad times better.

I was diagnosed with aplastic anemia, which causes the body to stop producing blood cells. The illness was sudden. In a short span of time I was unable to continue working and was required to visit the hospital for blood and platelet transfusions, two to four times per week. Within a matter of weeks, it felt like everything had been taken away, with no end in sight and no hope that I would be able to regain my previous life.

I allowed myself to let anger, fear and depression take over. I was so angry at God and the world that I lost my faith.

On one hospital visit, a friend, my brother and my mother were sitting with me. We were laughing, joking and remembering. I realized that though I may have been at the lowest point in my life, I was not alone. I realized that God had made sure that I had the love and support needed to not have to carry the weight alone. I let go of the anger and fear and put my trust and faith in His hands.

I saw and took advantage of the opportunity to build and strengthen my relationships with family and friends. Giving my complete faith and trust in God, I had light in my life again. I received the bone marrow transplant I needed, defying the high odds that I would not get such a high donor match.

I have completely recovered and remain fervent in the belief that when you put your trust in God, all things are possible.

Through the Valley

My Testimony of Making it to the Other Side

By June Rock

My testimony is a jigsaw puzzle of people, places and milestones, childhood playmates, Sunday School, university, wedding, Canada, jobs, vacations, childbirth, family. But the moment that is frozen in my head is the day my dear husband passed away.

My earliest memory is walking to church as a toddler. I remember sitting in church and tying a bow on my dress for the first time. I remember my mom taking us for a walk at night to the neighbourhood church and listening to the service outside the window. I remember my granny asking me to read the Bible to her when her sight was failing. I remember talking to my first best friend about God. I remember Llewyn and I having our engagement blessed in the office of Bethel Methodist Church (where I was confirmed) and Reverend Rock praying for us.

I remember when we moved to Canada my husband and I rented an apartment that was just five minutes away from a Methodist church, just like the one I had been raised in. I remember meeting my second best friend on the first visit to that church, and going to our Young People's Bible Study that she started. I remember taking my turn in the prayer circle thanking God for His blessings.

So, if God was with me in all those times leading up to my personal D-Day, giving me the foundation of hearing His word and learning to walk with Him, why then did I have to go through such a heart-breaking time? My answer is that I do not know. I have friends who have never known Christ and some who have walked away from Him, and they faced hardships too, so how is my life different? My response made the difference: I continued to turn to and lean on God.

Every time that I see a news story of a widowed family my heart breaks for that woman and for the family because I can still remember that day when I too faced that same news. I can remember the doctor coming into the waiting room, looking at our baby, what He said to me, my friends coming to find us, saying goodbye. I can still see people walking across the hospital parking lot and thinking that they are heading home but they did not know that my life has just turned upside down. I know why my memories of that day, and so many after, are in black and white – it was the darkest day of my life.

You may wonder if I can have a testimony today that has anything remotely positive. My answer is that *today* I do, because God carries me, just like in the Footprints poem. He was with me before, with me during, and is with me every moment since that terrible day. My valley seemed like a never-ending tunnel, but it got better, one footstep at a time. Some pains are gone, some remain even after 20 years: at birthdays, anniversaries, events in the family, mentions of "that hospital", but they don't flatten me like they used to. Showing the child that never knew her Dad just how much she is like him... I think that will *always* be hard.

I am sharing my story for anyone who has lost someone, anyone, where the pain hurts so much that you cry and cry and cry until there are no tears left. Your mind and body seem to be separate elements and your own voice seems to be coming from somewhere outside of you. **Proverbs 3:5-6** was always my favourite Proverb, and it became a motto to me: to lean on God and not on my own understanding and to let him direct my paths. God only knows that many days I did not understand what was happening or what I should be doing!

In those times, I was blessed that my family and friends held my hands up, like Aaron and Hur did for Moses in **Exodus 17:12**. But I also found that there are stories and verses in the Bible that speak to whatever situation that we are facing. I just had to search for the ones that applied to me and find those that soothed my spirit. I did not realize that I had so many bandages and blessings available to me until God started using them to bind my hurting mind, body and soul, and put me back together.

One of my favourite verses is **Philippians 4:13**, that we can do **all** things *through* Christ who strengthens us. I found out what "through Christ" meant when I would be doing chores and start to cry, or trying to pray and words would not come, or when all I could do was to clutch my Bible to my chest in order to fall asleep. Although you cannot see Him standing beside you or carrying you, I promise you that God is indeed right beside you.

Psalm 91 says that God "is my refuge and my fortress" and we can trust in Him when we need a sanctuary, when our walls come crumbling down. My testimony is about God and His ability to shield us from the worst of a storm and to build us up again, no matter what is in ruins at that moment.

Even if you did not have any bricks to start with, or if yours were broken during your tragedy, or even if you threw away your bricks in pain and frustration, the words in the Bible are freely available and apply to EVERYONE that God created. We can rebuild our temples. The healing process will start inside us, even though we may not see anything changing outside. **Matthew 7:7-8** tells the truth: we can ask and God will give, we can seek and He will let us find what we need, we can knock and He will open windows and doors and even build highways for us!

In **1 Peter 5:7** I was reminded that I can cast my cares on Him because He cares for me. So if you ask me, "Why me then, if God cares so much?" Once again I have no answer. I told myself over and over that I am a child of God. Do you know that you are too! I also know that it may seem cruel, even impossible, to say that we should get up and keep going when we are hurting and broken.

In the same way that a parent will hold a child who falls on the playground and then send him/her on their way to play outside again, so too Christ says to us – come for a hug, cry as much as you want and I'll wipe away your tears, then I'll put some ointment to heal the bruises and you can go out and play again. But we have to come to Him and ask for his help. If I had stayed hiding from God, He could not heal me or dry my tears or give me the hope that He has promised in **Jeremiah 29:11.** Your loss may not be through death, but betrayal and disappointment feel just the same!

Although we would prefer to be shielded from everything that is difficult, we can persevere and fight just as a baby does coming into this world. We are never without an advocate and God is the strength that we can depend on. **Psalm 27:14** reminded me to hold on to my courage and wait on the Lord. I just keep going, day by day by day, and now more than 20 years have passed. If you feel alone and abandoned, **Romans 8:35-39** reminds us that nothing can separate us from the love of Christ Jesus our Lord, so no matter what pains the world throws at us we can always survive if we choose to.

You may even consider that by surviving really well we are treading on the lions and adders that want us to fail (**Psalm 91**). We still have our own path to follow, much to do and much we can share with others. They can see through the way we handle our trials that God is truly *our Father* and *our Shepherd*. He will lead us in green pastures and restore our soul, as it says in **Psalm 23.**

Blessings, Faith, Miracles and Courage are free for us all, because they are already paid in full by our Lord Jesus Christ. We just have to use them, like tools in our kitchen or workshop:

- **Blessings** in big public things and blessings in small everyday things that will not mean a thing to anyone else. Everything is provided to lighten your path, so ask God to help you recognise them.
- **Faith** that will grow as each day passes, as you see God at work around you; but faith that is small like a mustard seed is also OK. God takes us as we are and with whatever talent we offer.
- **Miracles** are still available on request and happening in this age but we can only see them when we look with eyes of faith – so let's keep our lenses clean.
- **Courage** is there waiting, reaching out to us, so ask, seek and knock. Using one thumb and one finger is not enough. You have to grab your courage and hold on with both hands.

My testimony is that I am able to hold on to God to carry me through every day and every situation that I face as a widow with a family. Yes, I mean this in the *present* tense! It has been very hard but I am making it and you can make it too, breath by breath and day by day, regardless of what *your* personal tragedy has been.

God has given us many promises, and the very last words that Jesus spoke to each and every one of us are found in **Matthew 28:20,** *"I am with you always, even unto the end of the world."*

Perhaps this prayer will get you started:

Dear Father,

I am hurting and need your comfort and peace. You have promised that you are here so please give me the courage and faith to hold on to you. As it says in **Isaiah 40:31***, I want to renew my strength, to run and not be weary and to walk and not faint.*

Amen.

Qualities of a Good Lay Person

By Rev. Keith E. Lohnes

What makes an ideal lay person? Every pastor knows he/she cannot do the job alone in leading the church and ministering for the Lord. Each spirit-filled believer in Jesus receives at least one spiritual gift. A church can only thrive when lay people recognize and use their abilities and spiritual gifts for the Lord.

When Moses led the children of Israel in the building of the tabernacle as a place of worship, he recruited skilled tradespeople to help – Bezalel and Oholiab. They were not priests or religious workers, but had abilities vital in the building of the tabernacle. We read in **Exodus 31:1-6**

> *Then the Lord said to Moses, "See, I have chosen Bezalel son of Uri, the son of Hur, of the tribe of Judah, and <u>I have filled him with the Spirit of God, with wisdom, with understanding, with knowledge and with all kinds of skills</u> to make artistic designs for work in gold, silver and bronze, to cut and set stones, to work in wood, and to engage in all kinds of crafts. Moreover, I have appointed Oholiab, son of Ahisamak, of the tribe of Dan, to help him. Also I have given ability to all the skilled workers to make everything I have commanded you."*

No doubt they had learned those skills while in captivity in Egypt.

In **Acts 6** we read how leaders of the early church chose seven helpers to assist in the food distribution to the needy, widows, etc. **Acts 6:3** reads: *Brothers and sisters, choose seven men from* *among you who are known to be full of the Spirit and wisdom....* One of the seven was Stephen **(v.5)** *"...Stephen, a man full of faith and of the Holy Spirit."*

In these two Bible accounts, we see qualities emerging for laypersons serving the Lord: 1) willing to serve; 2) skills were consecrated to the Lord; 3) filled with the Spirit of God; 4) with wisdom and understanding; 5) with knowledge; 6) full of faith.

My father, Clarence Lohnes, grew up on the farm, never finished elementary school, never went to high school. But he loved to read good books, including some Christian books I still have in my collection. He served the church as an usher, treasurer and board member; he helped bring people to church and served in many other ways. He would sing duets with my mother. Often he arrived at church early to unlock the door and was the last to leave, making sure the building was secure. I remember him saying he had the gift of "helps".

When the church ran short of funds, he paid bills himself, even though he had a modest income. He would lead in family prayer, usually on Sunday afternoons, having worked shift during the week at a factory. He taught his three sons the value of work and duty and, by his life, demonstrated his faith in Jesus Christ. He insisted that we arrive on time for church. A favorite phrase of his was "if you are not five minutes early, you are late". I am blessed by his life and example.

You Are Never Alone

By Caroline G. Haynes

A man that hath friends must shew himself friendly: and there is a friend that sticketh closer than a brother.
Proverbs 18:24

I was feeling lonely once again when everyone else had gone off to work and school. There I lay across my bed thinking that I had not one friend I could call upon in my loneliness when the Lord spoke to my spirit and said, "I am your friend." Less than five minutes later the phone rang and there on the other end of the receiver was my friend Sabrina who said that she was just thinking of me.

God is so good to us. I needed to hear that Jesus is my friend. He is our friend always; He also knows when we need to hear the voice of someone we can see and touch with our senses.

Thank you, Jesus, for always being my friend; for sticking closer than a brother or sister. Thank you, God, for speaking your love and friendship through my friend Sabrina. Forgive me, Lord, for forgetting what a special friend you are to me.

Greater love hath no man than this, that a man lay down his life for his friends. Ye are my friends if ye do whatsoever I command you. Henceforth I call you not servants; for the servant knoweth not what his LORD doeth: but I have called you friends; for all things that I have heard of my Father I have made known unto you. **John 15:13-15**

...and lo I am with you always, even unto the end of the world.
Matthew 28:20

I have learned that I can depend on the Lord when no one else seems dependable. Jesus said He would never leave us or forsake us.

There were two devastating experiences in my life where I saw his faithfulness in keeping that promise. The first was as a young woman pregnant and alone. He proved his faithfulness to me even though I had been unfaithful to him. The second experience was five years later at the death of twin babies that my husband and I were expecting.

During both these experiences I cried out to the Lord in my despair, desperation and loneliness. It was then that I felt Him speak to my heart that He would be with me when there was no one to understand or stand beside me.

He was there then and is still here beside me today.

God's Awesome Love

By Isaac Burnett

In this reflection piece, I would like to testify to my experiences of God's love based on His faithfulness, the miracles He performed in my life and a blessing that He bestowed upon me. In doing so, I will discuss some challenges that proved these things to me. Eventually, it should be realized that He always surrounds us with His love and He manifests it by answering prayers and rewarding good deeds.

My earliest experience of God's love was through His faithfulness in response to His promise. As a reminder, He promised "not to leave nor forsake us" **(Hebrews 13: 5,6)**. This commitment was manifested in my life at an early age when all attending physicians despaired regarding my sickness and started preparing my parents for the worst. At that stage, the good Lord intervened and restored hope through the advice of an elderly doctor. This doctor advised the use of natural measures including herbal remedies and prayer. In response, my parents put aside anxiety and fear and instead exercised obedience, innovation and courage in carrying out the given advice.

In the long run, I was cured of my sickness, thanks to the healing power of prayer and the great work of my caregivers. Of course, the mystery of it all was the awesome power of God's love which was manifested through the keeping of His Promise. For that matter, I do believe that He did intervene and inspired my caregivers to do the things that were necessary to cure me of my ailment. Consequently, I have come to love and trust Him more.

Further on in life, His love was again experienced in the form of a miracle that He performed in my favour. Thinking about it, I am reminded that the good Lord works in mysterious ways in performing His wonders in our lives **(1 Corinthians 2:7)**. For that matter, I became convinced that on a certain occasion, only He could have inspired the stopping of a vehicle within seconds of a near fatal accident in which I was involved. My survival that day bore a keen resemblance to a divine intervention into my affairs. I recovered from that ordeal with the conviction that it was the love and mercy of a compassionate God that saved my life. As a result, I am humbled by His miracles and the mysterious ways in which He demonstrates them. They give me a sense of hope and redemption.

As I matured towards the middle years of my life, I again experienced the love of God through yet another miracle. It took place after our parents were laid to rest and their surviving children gathered to choose a caretaker for the few things that they left behind. During the conversations, the good Lord intervened in a remarkable way and revealed to us the right choice.

In following up, the siblings shook hands, hugged and greeted each other in a show of satisfaction with the outcome of events. In fact, the joy and happiness that overcame us served as testament to the awesome power of God's love and the unselfish way in which He choose to share it. I believe that on that day, it was His miracalous intervention upon the scene that removed all doubts, forged a peaceful settlement and resulted in continued family unity. For that matter, my siblings and I will always be grateful to Him for His watchful habit and miraculous practice.

Furthermore, a common belief is that whomever God blesses, no one can curse. The significance of this statement became real in my youth, when God's awesome love was experienced in the form of a special blessing. It came at a time when self-esteem was eroding and despair began to set in. Eventually, it served to restore needed confidence and re-kindled my courage. In reality, that blessing involved the obtaining of airline tickets and pocket money from a local promotional contest.

With that blessing, my father and I were able to travel and see the wonders of some cities within the Americas. As well, it enabled us, for the first time, to be flown above the clouds and experience some of the wonders of God's heavens. Looking back, I am reminded that everything takes place within its season **(Ecclesiastes 3:1-6)** and also, that each of us has our favourable day(s) **(Acts 17:26)**. Collectively, these ideas and experiences lead me to believe that my luck back then was a special blessing from God. Thus, in light of that and all else, I am forever grateful to Him.

I have shared with you a number of experiences that I do believe had divine connections and significance. Evidently, the incidents reflected God's faithfulness, miracles and blessings in my life. Hopefully, these incidents reveal my awareness of His grace and mercies towards me. Looking ahead, it is my desire that He will continue to guide and protect us all, both here and in the afterlife. Furthermore, using my experiences as telltale signs of God's love for us, we should try to remain strong in our faith and always wear His spiritual armour in order to fend off the devil. Eventually, we should be able to achieve absolute peace, love, joy and happiness.

God Opens Doors

By Ida Chatham

The Lord said to me, let your light so shine before men that they may see your good works and glorify your Father which is in heaven.

Matthew 5:16

My name is Ida Chatham. I am a member of the Bramalea Free Methodist Church. Before coming to Canada, I got married at an early age, and after that it was children. In those days, it wasn't easy to feed the kids and find things for school. I did not know how I made it, but **Proverbs 3:5**, says to "lean not on your own understanding". When I obeyed, the Lord opened the door for me. I was able to get a job at a school as a janitor from 1966 until I retired. My husband and I saw how God opened the doors of mercy for us.

Since moving to Canada, the Lord opened my eyes more clearly. I see so many things that the Lord has done for me. He is in control of my life and what He has done for me, He will do for you.

Amen.

* Sister Ida is over 80 years old

This is My Story

By Ronjel Elaine Stuart

Let me start with the chorus of this well known song **Blessed Assurance** written by Fanny J Crosby (1820-1915) which speaks of the assurance of being an "heir of salvation".

> *This is my story, this is my song,*
> *Praising my Savior all the day long.*
> *This is my story this is my song,*
> *Praising my savior all day long.*

Everyone has a story to tell whether we are aware of it or not. Telling your story will motivate others to open up (figuratively speaking), spiritually and emotionally, enhance your life, broaden your horizon, and help to reach out to others. We can also learn from each other's story. Each story has its advantages and disadvantages. No matter how negative a story might seem there is always something positive to gain from it. It is likened to a dark tunnel, which has a light at the end.

I, too, have a story and I feel proud and honored to tell my story. Let me introduce myself. My name is Ronjel Elaine Stuart (née Smith). I was born to parents Benjamin and Inez Smith on Tuesday, July 15, 1952, in a little remote village tucked away in the lush green hills of South East St. Ann in Alderton, Jamaica. I am the 15th of 17 children born to my parents.

I attended the Alderton All-Age School which is affiliated with the Alderton Methodist School. Classes were kept in the church building from Monday to Friday and the premises were prepared on a Friday afternoon for church service on Sunday. However, the school was moved to its existing location in September of 1960. I attended Claremont All-Age School for a short time, then went back to Alderton All-Age and then to Excelsior High School in Kingston. Excelsior is also affiliated with the Methodist Church.

After graduating from Excelsior I went to Church Teachers' College in Mandeville. This college is affiliated with the Anglican Church. I graduated in 1975 and then I went to Moneague College, where I graduated in 1990. When I emigrated to Canada I went to Everest College and was a member of the graduating Class of 2010.

My parents were Christians. My mother was a member of the Alderton Methodist Church and my father a member of the Alderton Seventh Day Adventist Church. Although we worship on different days we respected each other's worship time hence there was no conflict among us.

My siblings and I attended Sunday morning services and Sunday school in the evenings. It wasn't a case of whether or not we wanted to go to church, nor did we have a choice in what to wear. All we heard was "go and get ready for church and your clothes are on the bed". Rain or shine it was a must.

We received prizes every Christmas for attending Sunday School regularly. I was a member of the Young Adventures, Girls Guide, and junior choir. I always looked forward to Communion Sunday because after church service other children and I would go to the vestry for the leftover communion bread. These were little hard dough bread cubes baked by church members.

The Saturday before Harvest/Thanksgiving service I would help with the preparation and decoration of the church for harvest service. There were two services, one in the morning and the other in the afternoon.

I was christened one evening in my early teens at home by our minister. Being a child then I did not question the lateness for my christening. However, living in a Christian home I know now that I was already bless. I went to "preparation class" (now known as confirmation class) in my early 20s and became a member of the Alderton Methodist Church. I was proud and felt good to be taking communion. I continued to go to church regularly as well as to parties. I would party till early morning and then go to church. I thought all was well but did not realize then that I was just a church-goer.

During my second year at Church Teacher's College I had a mental breakdown and had to be away from college for two weeks. My sickness was on-and-off: feeling better today and sick tomorrow. During my sickness I prayed regularly but would dwell on my sins when I felt better. However, I did not know that the time would come when my God would start showing me signs.

One New Year's Eve I was in church as customary and left with a male and female friend for a party. He drove so fast that the car went out of control and almost ended in a shop. The people standing at the entrance had to run for safety. My only response was "Lawd God mi Dead (Jamaican Patois meaning "Lord God I am going to die.")

Another sign was when a youth club member died while giving birth. I said, "This could be me." Still I was not shaken. It was not until my late 20s that I realize I needed to turn my life around, so I recommitted my life to the Lord. I am a firm believer in miracles, and I can sing this chorus:

He's a miracle working God,
He's a miracle working God.

My God is a wonder,
My God is a miracle,
He's a miracle working God.

Author Unknown

In 2008, I was on vacation in Jamaica and experienced abdominal pains. On my return to Canada I went to see my family doctor who in turn sent me to see a specialist. I was sent for a myriad of tests. A cyst was found on my liver, which was benign. I was slated to do surgery on my liver and would lose part of it. I was sent by the surgeon to see another specialist. More tests were done but I have not heard from him again.

During my sickness and tests, friends, relatives and I prayed and declared healing in my body. Who could it be but God the great healer? He is my deliverer because He delivered me. When we pray there should be no doubts but just believe because all things are possible. My walk with God is a very challenging one and when I am attacked by the devil I always rebuke him and let him know that he is a loser and my God is victorious. *"Jesus paid it all, all to Him I owe."* The Bible is my source of strength and inspiration.

The first time I stepped into the pew at BMFC, I knew that this was the church that the Lord wanted me to attend. There was a special welcome that awaited me. The fellowship here is beyond measure. We share each other's joy, pain, sorrow and grief. What a way to experience and share God's love! No wonder the songwriter, Frederick M. Lehman (1868-1953) wrote, *"The love of God is greater far than pen or tongue can ever tell."*

Our Testimonies

We pull down every stronghold and claim deliverance and victory in the name of Jesus. To sum it all up, we are our brothers' and sisters' keepers. We are a multicultural church that reaches out and meets the needs of people in Brampton and beyond. If you need a home away from home BMFC is the place to be.

Everyone has a gift from God and this should be used to the glory of God. You may not be a preacher but if you clean the church and do it well, that is a gift from God. I use my gift to usher and also to help mould the lives of our children at Sunday school. We have a very rich package that enables the children to express themselves through drama, song, play, dialogue, and arts and craft. I also extend my gift beyond BFMC. My monetary gift is sent to Alderton Methodist Church (my alma mater) to help spread the gospel through missionary work. My gift of the Samaritan Shoe Box helps to spread the gospel to children in other countries.

I am very thankful for the way that I was brought up by my parents. There were many things that my siblings and I had to go without but we were grateful and thankful for the little that they could afford. Above all we were given love which is the greatest. Thanks mama and papa. May your souls rest in peace and light perpetual shine upon you.

I would like to end my story with some lines of the song written by Joseph M. Scriven (1820-1886):

> *What a friend we have in Jesus*
> *All our sins and griefs to bear!*
> *What a privilege to carry,*
> *Everything to God in prayer.*

Have we trials and temptations?
Is there trouble anywhere?
We should never be discouraged
Take it to the Lord in prayer.

Are we weak and heavy laden
Cumbered with a load of care?
Precious Savior, still our refuge
Take it to the Lord in prayer.

The writer goes on to say in the song that through prayer, all our sins, griefs, sorrows, weaknesses and cares are resolved in One who is not only our friend, but also our shield, our peace, our refuge and our solace.

To all my readers this is "My Story". Special thanks to the Big Bold Book Idea committee for your inspiration and encouragement that has motivated me to tell my story.

To God be the glory.

When God Is Near

By Unita Sam-Darling

When God is near, Sarah is not just a menopausal old woman of 80, barren. Sarah by faith conceived, gave birth to Isaac and became the mother of a whole nation blessed by God.

When God is near, Esther is not just a lovely young lady, built only to capture the Persian King's fancy. She is recorded for her heroic acts – as a young woman filled with faith, she gained courage and conviction to risk her life and thus saved the Jewish nation from impending annihilation.

When God is near, Naomi is not just an old woman bereft of all her sons and husband. But by faith, Ruth, her Moabite daughter-in-law, through love, compassion and obedience to Naomi, her Jewish mother-in-law, secured the hand of marriage to Boaz, a prince of the Jewish nation, thus starting the Davidic line of covenanted kings. We read that Jesus, born of David's line, shall sit on the throne of his father David. He is King of Kings and Lord of Lords, Son of the Almighty God – God Incarnate who dwelt among us.

You say that you are just a woman. Look! The rainbow is just an arch of pretty colours, yet whenever we see it, we remember God's promise that he will not drown the world again **(Genesis 9)**. Sometimes, it is not just the look of the thing itself that is the worthiest. For instance, though the rainbow does not cease to captivate our attention each time it appears in the sky, we should not forget that it is the symbol of God's grace.

Women, you and I are often too concerned about the exterior appearance, which is not bad, if taken in perspective. But do you know that when God is near you are a symbol of God's beacon of light to your generation?

The Longer our Battle

By Monique Peynado

I knew a young man who was a very loving and caring individual. He was an amazing son, brother and friend. His name meant warrior or one who fights the struggle. He definitely had a battle in life to fight, but due to internalized problems and extenuating circumstances, the battle was lost. He died on May 13.

It eventually dawned on me. I realized that we are all warriors fighting the battle of life. We all have personal issues and problems that we have to deal with. Problems in which some of us prevail and some of us don't.

We interact with all kinds of people on a daily basis. We exchange smiles and polite gestures to promote an attitude of happiness. Many times though, our outward actions are not a true reflection of how we feel on the inside. In reality we feel lonely and helpless deep down for whatever reason.

At times we may feel weak or incompetent. We feel as though we are not strong enough to fight our battles and through this we allow the struggle to get the best of us.

But what I want to leave with you today is this: No matter how big your fight is, remember that there is a bigger being out there who is capable of removing all the pain and anguish from your life. There is a popular saying that goes: "Don't tell God how big your struggles are; tell your struggles how big your God is."

So I charge you today to never give up the fight. Keep pressing on and remember that the longer your battle, the stronger your victory.

Let us pray.

> *Heavenly Father, we come to you at this time to pray for those who struggle with internal issues that only You alone can understand.*
>
> *Help us to realize that at our lowest times in our lives You are there to be our strength and refuge in our time of trouble. Help us to remember that in our daily struggles You will take away our sorrow in return for Your goodness and mercy if we look to You. Bless us with the strength to continue to persevere and grant us a sense of peace in knowing that You will never leave us. Send Your angels down to guide our steps and protect our paths.*
>
> *In Your name we pray. Amen.*

My Blessings, Faith, Miracles and Courage

This is my story, praising my Saviour all the day long!

By Sister V

WOW! A great idea was presented to us as a church family to collectively contribute our stories of **B**lessings, **F**aith, **M**iracles and **C**ourage towards a book that will bless us and the future generations that follow. God planted this seed in a sister's mind and we pray that our stories will bless all those who are privileged to read our book.

To begin, over the years at BFMC I have volunteered in various capacities such as nursery helper, teller, board member, hospitality caterer, a supporter of the women's ministry and also part of the Connections Team. In 2006 cancer attacked my body but not my soul. I would therefore like to share that story from the perspectives of Blessings, Faith, Miracles and Courage. Eventually, I would hope that my testimony inspires and motivates you to trust God and believe that with Him all things are possible. Yes, you can have a life after cancer. Rest if you must but do not quit! Be persistent, brave and hopeful.

Now, with a focus on **Blessings,** God has proven many times over how much He loves us and I truly felt and embraced that awareness more sincerely after a diagnosis with cancer. In fact, I literally began counting my many blessings. For when the devil tried to tell me that the cancer was terminal and that there was no hope, I challenged him in a less than polite manner. Indeed, I told Satan to go back to hell where he belongs and take his hands off God's blessed child (a daughter of the King). He did just that and, as a consequence, I am still around to experience God's grace, love and mercy.

As far as **Faith** in God, it was heightened when on a daily basis I exercised it through my words, thoughts and deeds. Moreover, I continually sing hymns that boost my soul. In fact, one of those hymns was my mom's favourite before it became mine as well. It is entitled, **My Faith Looks Up to Thee.** Whenever I hear that song, it further strengthens my faith and hope in the God I trust.

Turning to **Miracles**, we often hear of or know someone who said he/she experienced one of them. Well, it is true that miracles still happen to those who believe! Over the years, my many medical health checks have taught me, and I am still learning, how to adequately monitor my personal health. Through that experience, I have certainly encountered my share of miracles but there was one especially that stood out and it helped to change my life in a positive way.

Nonetheless, in recent times I encountered some more challenges with one of my lungs. In response, I prayed specifically to God and asked Him to grant that the accumulated fluid would be removed by the time of my follow-up visit to the doctor. Oh, what a mighty God we serve? I went on to believe, pray and expect a miracle. On the morning of my medical appointment I kept hope alive by continuing to expect my miracle and as you might guess, I did receive it. Upon examination, the specialist said to me, "Your last X-ray had shown excess fluid in one of your lungs, but today's x-ray shows that the fluid has decreased." THAT WAS A WOW MOMENT FOR ME!!! My spontaneous reply was: "I've got my miracle!"

Then when it came to dealing with **Courage**, I was always encouraged and embraced by my biological family. (May God bless each one of them). They supported and lifted me up on a daily basis with their prayers, love and good deeds. Furthermore, I shall forever be appreciative of, and also extremely grateful for, the loving and unwavering support of my siblings and their families. As well, my son has been and continues to be the bright star in my heart and home. Collectively, the courage of these well-wishers goes far in sustaining and supporting me. Again, thanks to the good Lord who caused them to show such virtue of kindness towards me in my sickness. I am forever indebted to all of them.

Finally, my gratitude goes out to a number of contributors to my causes in life. The first of them is my BMFC family who have been my alternate family for over 20 years. You will never understand the depth of gratitude that flows from my heart to you for being there, welcoming and warmly embracing me every Sunday as I continue to worship with you. You prayed for and supported me during my time of chemotherapy and radiation and even after surgery. Your prayers, understanding and support helped me "to keep on, keeping on!"

Next, to the worship leaders and teams: may God bless you as your music continues to inspire. You remind me how good it is to enter and be present in the house of God! Being part of BFMC's family continues to be an encouraging and uplifting experience for me. From the pulpit all the way to the back pew I am so blessed. Thank you all. Many of you continue to pray without ceasing for me and my son. My spiritual sisters and brothers, thank you for your unwavering love and support.

Now, as a seven-year past director of **The Olive Branch of Hope Cancer Support Group** in the Peel Region, I will be amiss if I do not thank both the BFMC Board and Pastor Doug. They welcomed, supported and allowed us to host our monthly meetings and Christmas group luncheons at the church over the years. In that same vein, Pastor Rusty encouraged us with ideas and views regarding a larger picture for the group. Therefore, my gratitude and appreciation go out to both the Pastors and the Board.

As well, to my assistant director, Audrey Isaacs, the many facilitators and supporters from BFMC; you have blessed us tangibly and intangibly. Therefore, I and the other survivors thank you from the bottom of our hearts.

To the brothers (Trevor Hitchman and Louis Isaacs), who were brave enough to volunteer and work with an all-ladies' cancer group, we applaud you for your audacity, expertise and commitment to us and the cause. God bless you abundantly. Of course, my sincere thanks to everyone who supported and attended our fundraising events. May God bless and keep you. Again, thanks for caring and partnering with us.

Last but not least, to the future generation of BFMC, I implore you to *"aspire to inspire before you expire"* (**Eugene Bell Jr. 2011**).

Live, Love and Laugh.

Blessings always.

Reflections of Faith, Love, Family and Friendship

By Trevor Hitchman

When one thinks of one's journey in life, the thoughts usually are based on such things as childhood experiences, the teen years, schooling, jobs, marriage, family and good friends, to name a few. Sometimes, in the mix of these thoughts, life-changing experiences can challenge one's reason of human existence and if there is **one God** who knows the beginning and outcome of one's destiny. That is why in my off time from daily chores I take some time to reflect on some experiences, particularly a life-changing one I had many years ago that strengthened my faith in God.

I grew up in a Christian family, as did my wife, Yvonne. Going to church and Sunday School was the "norm". To refuse was non-negotiable. Therefore, except for a brief part of early childhood, our entire lives have seen us as members of the Methodist Church from Jamaica to Canada. My Christian upbringing was exciting and edifying because I learned to read the Bible, **"my first Big Book"**, and that helped me to understand the sermons of many pastors. This was the early foundation that facilitated my faith in God; that it was normal to demonstrate this faith with prayer, worship and praise, and thank Him for humankind existence.

In fact, I must reflect on a life-changing experience that occurred on May 26, 2004, when I survived a multi-vehicle accident in Ann Arbor, Michigan, USA. Many people were injured but my injuries were the worse – they were catastrophic – so paramedics took me to Michigan University Hospitals and Health Centers, located about two miles from the accident scene. Doctors performed seven major surgeries, scheduled at different times due to the severity of the injuries, as well as made dedicated efforts to prevent any amputation of limb, that is, my left leg.

The entire experience lasted for ten months that involved healthcare providers shuttling me between the hospital and rehabilitation centre for each scheduled surgery. Every movement by me was assisted by healthcare providers because I was "living" on my back during that time. There were times when despair came over me and I wondered if my life would continue in a wheelchair with a permanent disability. Fear of that circumstance set in and I prayed to God to let me walk again, for I believed He had more things for me to do. In the summer of 2005, surgery number eight was performed at St. Michael's Hospital in Toronto.

Sometimes I felt alone but "not really alone". For example, there were the regular telephone calls, letters, and get-well cards. My family – comprising my wife Yvonne, our two sons, daughter-in-law and late cousin Louise – travelled each week to visit me in the hospital or the Rehab Centre. An older brother Kenneth and wife, Nellie, from the UK; sister Ina and husband Desmond from the USA, and in Toronto my late oldest sister, Bearon, including other siblings from near and far in Canada made several visits and prayed at my bedside. However, most times I was heavily sedated so this last part was mentioned to me much later. Now, with some limitations, I can walk again and am thankful to my God.

There is a saying that people only need five great things in their lives. I wonder, what are these things, and would they provide a full and satisfied life? Perhaps, but I believe I was blessed with many more. For me, one of these "great things" must be my many friends from Montreal and the Wesleyan Church in Toronto, some who stepped in and helped Yvonne at a time of need while I was in the hospital. Again, I was thankful and grateful for the help. I still do, because I can remember.

That was my life-changing experience and I believe I could not have survived it without God's mercy and the constant care and support of my loving wife, Yvonne.

Faith Roots: An Enlightening Discovery

By Esther Sarpong

"*H*ere O my Lord, I see Thee face to face."

"What does that mean?" the little girl asks herself as she listens to the congregation sing and watches the group of people kneeling at the altar. She is tired and hungry. All she wants at this point is to go home, eat her lunch and get ready for her weekly Sunday visits with her maternal grand mom, Granny Jane. Instead she has to wait for her parents to finish the communion service before they can leave the church.

The scenario described above took place in a Methodist church. Though frustrating to the little girl at the time, it is one of the cherished memories she now has of her childhood church along with other memories such as the priest telling Bible stories each Sunday.

The little girl is me. As a young member of Samaria West African Methodist Church in Freetown, Sierra Leone, my childhood memories of church are filled with the happy times I spent worshipping with my family and other families at our beloved Samaria church.

Reflecting on my childhood Methodist experience back home vis-a-vis my adult experience at Bramalea Free Methodist, the word "Free" was what caught my attention. But before I delve into any discussion of these two experiences, a little background is necessary for readers to see why I chose to write on this particular topic.

When I arrived in Canada as a student almost 30 years ago, one of the first things I did was to scout around my Bay/Bloor neighbourhood in search of a Methodist Church of which I could become a member. My search was fruitless! Desperate for a church community that resembled the one I had back home, I eventually walked into The Church of the Redeemer, an Anglican church at the corner of Bloor Street and Avenue Road, where I was warmly welcomed. For the next five years I attended service there regularly.

In 1993, I married and moved to the Lawrence and Black Creek community. When I became a mom, the journey downtown to the Church of the Redeemer became almost impossible. Our family then joined the congregation of St. David's Anglican Church at Lawrence and Jane, where we actively worshipped until our move to Brampton in the spring of 2000. My search for a Methodist church started afresh. After several visits to many churches, we finally found Bramalea Free Methodist. I was overjoyed. At last I had found a Methodist church. We loved the warm church community and the vibrant Sunday school program. I felt a sense of belonging.

Then something caught my attention.

It was the word "Free". As a child in Freetown, I had attended a Methodist church; now Bramalea was called a "Free Methodist church. What's the difference? My curiosity pulled at me. Why was it called "Free Methodist"? Back home in Freetown, there were no "Free" Methodist churches! So I started a little digging. What I found was enlightening, so enlightening that I wish my grandmother, my parents and all the adults who had raised me Methodist, were still alive for me to share my findings with them.

I wonder what THEY would have made of my findings, given the fact that they worshipped so sincerely as "Methodists". Ironically Freetown had been founded in 1787 through the joint efforts of certain British abolitionists and the then British colonial government, as a home for freed slaves who had settled in Nova Scotia, but had expressed the desire to return to Africa from where their ancestors had originally been taken.

Nonetheless, O reader, if not yet acquainted with what makes the Free Methodist church "Free" you might be tempted to do a little digging of your own. Here, however, is what I learned from my own digging.

The Free Methodist Church has a rich heritage:

The Free Methodist church has its origins in the Methodist church founded by John Wesley. It was established in August 1860 in New York and Illinois at the time when the abolition of slavery was being hotly debated. It quickly spread across the entire North American continent. This new found church was similar to its mother church in that it sought to maintain the warm-hearted biblical message and lifestyle of the original Methodist church. However, its founders based this new church on certain distinct principles that set it apart from the original church and made it unique in its own right. These distinguishing features include but are not limited to the following:

Opposition to Slavery:

Free Methodists were opposed to slavery in America. Unlike the Methodist church which failed to take a stand against slavery, Free Methodists sought to eradicate and abolish slavery in the Americas and assisted slaves to escape to Canada through the Underground Railroad system.

Opposition to the practice of renting and selling church pews:

Methodists had a widespread practice of renting and selling church pews which relegated those who could not afford renting or buying pews to sit at the back of the church. Free Methodists advocated free seats for all and called instead for tithes and offerings to assist in paying for the church's ministries.

Freedom in Worship:

Free Methodists emphasized freedom of worship, rather than the formalism which characterizes worship in the Methodist church. As I stated in my introduction, one of the most frustrating experiences for me as a little girl, was having to wait for my parents to partake of Communion after an already formal and very lengthy worship time. From church to church and from congregation to congregation a variety of worship styles can be found. Yet the central point of worship in all Free Methodist churches is to glorify God and receive Biblical instruction commonly called Bible Study. In this respect God is worshipped in spirit and in truth.

People with a Mission:

Free Methodists are people with a mission. Their mission is to spread the good news to all, so that people will become whole through the forgiveness of Christ and live a holy life according to the teachings of Jesus Christ. Those who respond to this call are invited to become members who are prepared for ministry in their community and in the world. This can be vividly seen in Bramalea Free Methodist church's Mission Statement, which states that the church is "a diverse people moving with one mind in cheerful, humble obedience to further the mission and Kingdom of God in Brampton and beyond".

Devoted Global Christians:

Free Methodists are committed to spreading the gospel throughout their community. Free Methodist Christian colleges, universities and Bible Study programs train and equip men and women for Christian ministry all over the world.

Students of the Bible:

The basis of faith for Free Methodists is the bible. Free Methodists strive to live their lives according to the teachings of the Bible. Free Methodists churches are dedicated to exposing its members to the teachings of the Bible so they will grow in grace and faith.

Christian Witnesses:

Free Methodists make it a goal to be true representatives of Christ in their daily lives. This is manifested in the way they live their lives and in sharing the scriptures with others through outreach and bible study programs.

Generous Christians:

Every year Free Methodists donate financially and in other ways. They are usually at, or near the top, in per capita giving of tithes and offerings. Their love of God leads them to follow His example to care for and be generous to others. Their compassionate outreach to the needy is seen not only in local congregations, but also in institutional ministries such as visits to hospitals and prisons and caring for inmates in women's shelters and assisting the general public with needs which Christians can help to meet.

After researching and discovering what the Free Methodist Church was all about, why it was founded and what it stood for, I was able to gain a deeper understanding of the Methodist church I grew up in. I now understand some of the differences between the Methodist and the Free Methodist ways of worship

Things which I did not understand as a little girl now made sense to me. I came to a deeper understanding and appreciation of the formalities that were observed and practiced at my childhood church, especially on important Sundays such as Easter and New Year Sunday; why the dress code was so strict and formal, why the choristers had to wear cassocks and surplices, sing anthems and lead the congregation in chanting the canticles. I understand why certain people occupied certain pews Sunday after Sunday and seemed resentful if they had to share it with others. I got to appreciate Bramalea Free Methodist Church- its missions, its mission statement, ministries, outreach programs and all its other activities and engagements.

I was also able to somehow appreciate the true meaning of what being a "Free Methodist" is all about and why Free Methodists broke away from the Methodist church. I am delighted to have found Bramalea Free Methodist Church. Had it not been for BFMC, I probably would never have done this research. In my journey as a Christian, I have grown in faith, knowledge and insight in terms of what truly makes a church, a church – a community of diverse, compassionate Christians, committed to spreading the Gospel, reaching out to the needy and less fortunate, and standing up against the injustices and inequalities that plague our communities, our nation and our world.

I wish I knew what I now know when I was a little girl growing up blissful and innocent in my Methodist Church in Freetown. I am left to wonder and continue my digging on who founded the West African Methodist Church. Did they know of the founding of the Free Methodist Church in the Americas? What were the philosophy and the mission behind the founding of the West African Methodist church in West Africa? Had the members of the West African Methodist Church themselves at that time given any serious thought as to why they had chosen to become members of the West African Methodist church.

I wonder…

If only my Granny Abigail was still alive… if only.

How a Women's League Meeting Led Me to Christ

By Ida Chatham

Therefore, if any man be in Christ he is a new creature: old things are passed away; behold, all things are become new.

2 Corinthians 5:17

That scripture verse speaks to how I was led to the Lord. The president of the Women's League at my church would stop me on Sundays to invite me to one of their meetings. I always promised but never turned up. However, one Wednesday night I got the urge to attend. I did not know it then, but the Lord was waiting for me.

Then and there, I gave my heart to the Lord Jesus. I was never the same after that and I never missed a meeting since. The Lord blessed me so abundantly that there was no way I was going to turn back. Praise the Lord.

I will end this story with one of my favourite choruses:

> *Running over, running over,*
> *My cup is full and running over;*
> *Since the Lord saved me, I'm as happy as can be,*
> *My cup is full and running over.*
>
> **Seth Sykes (1931)**

* Sister Ida is over 80 years

Fix Your Eyes on Jesus

By Christa Ball

Perhaps this has happened to you. You are suddenly struck with inspiration and you feel compelled to take that leap of faith. This is what I felt like when Dennis, my husband, told me about going into Ministry. We were so excited! Dennis started school and we started making plans about leaving his business. I remember us dreaming about the places God would take us and the impact we would make on the people around us.

Then something happened. I remembered that I didn't have a degree and I thought pastors' wives typically knew how to play the piano and are great singers and speakers. I wondered what would people expect from me. Were they expecting Martha Stewart? Mother Teresa? I am neither of them! I started to worry about where God would move us. What if He moved us somewhere scary?

I also wondered how we would get by financially with my husband starting a new career, and I started to scramble. I made an impulsive decision to buy a rental property thinking that would be a good safety net and our lives would remain comfortable. However, that lifeboat turned into the Titanic and we ended up running away from the landlord business at a great loss financially. How did I go from being excited about God's plan to drowning in my insecurities and doubts?

I imagine this is how Peter must have felt after stepping out of the boat (**Matthew 14:22-36**). He started out excited to meet Jesus on the water, only to find he was sinking. I picture him clawing at the waves looking to grab hold of them. I see him kicking his feet trying to find a foothold with no success. I hear him calling to his friends, only they were helpless to save him. But then, his eyes lock onto Jesus who is still standing on top of the water and Peter calls to him!

Then I heard Jesus speak to me as he spoke to Peter, "Why did you doubt?" "Why did I turn to the waves for help?" "Why would I think that money, talents or power would help me?" My problem began when I shifted my thoughts from God to my fears. There was no reason for me to struggle! Nothing had happened yet! I was so stuck on "what if" that I made some terrible decisions that were all based on fear of the unknown. **Hebrews 12:2** says:

> *Let us fix our eyes on Jesus, the author and perfecter of faith, who for the joy set before Him endured the cross, scorning its shame, and sat down at the right hand of the throne of God.*

Jesus is the author of our lives. He writes our future and we can trust him! He will take our hand and pull us out of the water. He will guide us when the way is unknown.

Dear Lord,

You are the author and perfecter of our faith! Thank You that You are in control and that You are trustworthy. You are faithful and strong and You will guide us through unknown waters. Amen!

* Christa is the wife of our current Pastor, Dennis Ball

Raising Awareness About Sickle Cell Disease

By Louis Isaacs

I first became involved with the sickle cell disease by donating funds through United Way to Camp Jumoke.

Simply put, sickle cell disease, is a blood disorder disease where the red blood cells stick together and are abnormal in shape compared to a normal cell, which is round. Both parents have to carry the trait in order for a child to be born with the disease.

No longer is it known as a disease that only affects the Black race. It is a disease that affects people from the Mediterranean, India, Latin America, South America, the Caribbean, Middle East, Sri Lanka and Africa. People who suffer from the disease can experience kidney, heart, liver and spleen problems.

Camp Jumoke is a summer camp which caters to kids affected by the disease. The camp is run by volunteers from the medical profession, social workers and other volunteers. The kids are taught how to cope with this dreadful disease (of which there is no cure) and life skills, while interacting with other kids like themselves. Camp Jumoke receives no monies from government and relies solely on donations and fundraisers to function. It is the only one of its kind in Canada.

As time went by I became more than a donor. I became a volunteer participating in fundraising events such as the annual bowl-a-thon, walk-a-thon and gala. Then I became a committee member. Over the years of my involvement I have been privileged to help bring awareness to the cause and the organization and lend my time wherever possible.

I became a member of the Sickle Cell Association Group of Ontario (SCAGO) and the Sickle Cell Disease Association of Canada (SCDAC). I have been a delegate for both organizations advocating at the provincial and federal levels of governments for a standard protocol in treating sickle cell patients at hospitals province-wide and to develop a National Health policy for Canada. A sickle cell registrar was also important for both groups in order to track and know how many sickle cell patients there are provincially and nationally. Awareness is part of the mandate of both organizations.

Becoming an advocate afforded me the opportunity to help bring awareness to the community through public speaking in churches in the GTA. I spoke with our former Pastor "Rusty" Crozier about my involvement in sickle cell and he encouraged me to use this as my ministry. Knowing that my passion was advocating for the awareness of sickle cell disease he inspired me to address the congregation many times. I did so through DVDs, presentations and pamphlets. These presentations were done on Sickle Cell Day (June 19) and in Sickle Cell month (September) The reception from the congregation was always encouraging and many people would remark that they knew of a relative or a friend who died from this painful disease and wanted to get involved.

I wish to thank Pastor Rusty for empowering and allowing me to bring awareness to others and encouraging them to know their status before starting a family.

From these events a partnership was developed between Camp Jumoke and BFMC Church. For the past two years, BFMC Board has approved the usage of the church hall to host the annual

Sickle Cell Christmas Kids' party, of which I am extremely thankful. Camp Jumoke and SCAGO jointly sponsored the first Christmas party event. In 2015, they were joined by a third sickle cell organization, the Sickle Cell Association of Ontario (SCAO). Camp Jumoke and SCAGO recognized BFMC's contribution with a Community Award Plaque on December 13, 2014. This plaque is currently on display in the church foyer.

Thanks to the many ladies of the church for their donations to the parties, and to Alex McFarlane for being Santa Claus both years. I wish to also express my gratitude to the many members of BFMC who have sponsored me for the bowl-a-thon and walk-a-thon fundraising events.

Finally, people are often times reluctant to admit being affected or carriers of the disease as society attaches a stigma to it, which should not be so since the disease is not contagious. Awareness and knowing how to manage this disease are two key factors in coping. I implore everyone, especially young couples planning to raise families, to become aware of their status by consulting with their family physicians.

Dear Lord,

Thank you for the opportunity to use our gifts in many ways. In so doing, we are continuing the legacy of your Son, Jesus Christ.

Special Words in a Successful Marriage

By Rev. Keith E. Lohnes

Gael and I have been blessed with a successful and happy marriage for over 50 years. We started dating during our high school years, and from the beginning made our faith in Christ central to our relationship. We have discovered that happy and harmonious relationships are far more important than wealth, fame, power and status.

During a wedding ceremony I performed at Bramalea Free Methodist Church in 2015, I shared some truths from the scripture and simple principles of "special words" for a happy and successful marriage. I pass them on for your blessing and encouragement. Above all, be true to your marriage vows.

Wisdom from God's word – Ephesians 4:1-7

Apostle Paul writing:

> *As a prisoner for the Lord, then, I urge you to live a life worthy of the calling you have received. <u>Be completely humble and gentle; be patient, bearing with one another in love. Make every effort to keep the unity of the Spirit through the bond of peace.</u> There is one body and one Spirit, just as you were called to one hope when you were called; one Lord, one faith, one baptism; one God and Father of all, who is over all and through all and in all. But to each one of us grace has been given as Christ apportioned it.*

Special Words in a Successful Marriage

1. **I Love You** – Say it frequently, regardless of feelings and make sure your actions and your words are spoken out of love. God is Love.

2. **Forgive Me** – When you're wrong, admit it; ask forgiveness. This applies to both men and women!

3. **I Forgive** – When your spouse asks forgiveness, you should forgive. Each should endeavor with God's help not to repeat mistakes. Remember Jesus said we must forgive 70 x 7. Don't allow anger and resentment to control your thoughts. Forgiveness is vital – we need God's help to fulfill this. (The Lord's Prayer). In a successful marriage each helps the other to become a better person.

4. **Thank you** – Remember common courtesy, appreciation. Vital!

5. **Let's Pray** – Prayer is a vital part of a happy marriage. Make God the centre of your home, your marriage and family. Invite Jesus Christ to be your Saviour and Lord. Teach your children and guide them in Christ's way. Be part of a dynamic Christian church, where there is good Bible teaching, fellowship and love.

Our Testimonies

Tribute to Gran

By Bri-Anne Smith

This was a tribute paid to Verna Burke at her home-going on July 29, 2015. She was a member of the BFMC family.

Friends and family, I'd like to thank you for coming out to support us during this time. You have laughed with us, cried with us, provided for us and cared for us and it's overwhelmingly beautiful to know that so many people are with us in the worst of times as they are during the best.

On November 30, 1943, one of the world's greatest women was born – Gran! You may know her as Verna Burke, but I've known her as my grandmother. She was "mom" to three beautiful daughters, grandmom to six grandchildren and five great-grands, sister to 17 siblings, and Oprah to the rest at the 12 Laurelcrest building.

On the day that Gran lost consciousness, she was having a GREAT day. She called my mom early in the morning to request five bottles of menthol for her friend. She visited her friends and went to the pool, not once but twice. Now, I don't know if it was because of her sexy new bathing suit – but I do know that it was causing quite a stir. Now let me tell you about this bathing suit. It was a red gold and orange floral piece. It crossed over the bust and cinched at the waist. Well, when someone asked where Gran got this extravagant bikini from. She says "I ain' tellin' she!" (This is Barbadian dialect meaning "I am not telling her.")

Gran was an integral part of our building's community. She went to the council meetings, and was at every potluck and every barbecue. Gran knew who was on vacation, who was moving out, who just had a baby, and who had a hip replacement last Friday at 3:07 p.m. You could find her in the lobby, down by the pool and in the mall on Thursdays.

Residents had to pray they didn't see her in the elevator. Are you not a morning person? Do you feel awkward making conversation in the elevator? Are you a generally grumpy person? TOO BAD – Gran's gonna talk to you! And you better respond too, before she says "I tek up my good mout to tell wunna mornin' and wunna playing great?" (Barbadian dialect which translates, "I take the time to tell you good morning and you are too posh to answer me.")

These little outbursts did not make it easy for her Canadian friends. Her Bajan (Barbadian) ramblings – sometimes understood and sometimes not – were welcomed and expected by friends close to her.

As I've heard countless times over the past few weeks – she was a great friend. Mom and I used to tease her about being a "phone-a-holic" because she was on the phone 24/7. But I've come to learn that she was untangling hearts while she tied up the phone lines. She called people morning, noon and night to make sure they were okay, to listen to their stories and impart her new-found Dr. Oz knowledge.

In our family, Gran was the matriarch. Loving her was not a question – she offered copious amounts of ice cream to children and adults alike. She could cook up a storm – cou & salt fish, lamb chops, sweetbread, homemade fries, fishcakes, bakes and sugar cakes were just a few of her extensive talents.

Despite her pain, she would find the time to take care of others. She could not help but do her utmost. She would stay over with friends who were ill and alone; she would bring soup to people who weren't feeling well; she would watch people's cats and plants while they were away. She taught us how to be selfless and put others before ourselves. She taught us to love in a way that went beyond understanding. It was undoubtedly a Christ-like love.

Every morning before she got out of bed she would give thanks to God for seeing another day, and as she rose she would read her **Daily Bread** (sometimes screaming it out to me as I got ready for school or work). In all of her years, Gran's faith in Jesus Christ brought her through situations that were more than the average human being could bear. After everything she went through, she came out smiling and singing her little song:

> *Don't let nobody steal your joy,*
> *Don't let nobody steal your joy,*
> *Don't let nobody steal your joy,*
> *You got joy, joy, joy.*
>
> **Author Unknown**

As we learn how to continue in life without Gran by our sides, I've made a list of some of the things that Gran lived by.

1. **"Don't be afraid of nobody; all people is people."** – It doesn't matter what position someone holds, how much or how little money they make. At the end of the day you don't have to fear them because they are made up of flesh and bones just like you.

2. **"I'm alive!"** – Everyday is a blessing and you're lucky to be alive. Sure, everything could feel like it's falling apart but you're alive. You've been given another day to make the most out of your life and see the beauty in the world.

3. **"Always make up your bed and wear clean underwear."** – This is self-explanatory. You never know who may come over to the house and you never know what may happen outside the house. You don't want the paramedics to have to take care of you in dirty underwear, you know.

4. **"Come have some ice cream (or insert another sweet thing)."** – Life is too short to limit yourself. Yes, everything should be done in moderation but you deserve to taste all the good that life has to offer, so you go ahead. Have yourself that cup of pistachio ice cream.

5. **"Life isn't fair but God is good."** – This is the most important lesson and also the most difficult to learn. It's hard to decipher why certain things happen in life.

No, not everything is fair. I never imagined losing the woman I had shared a room with for the past 20 years of my life. I knew it had to happen but there would never be a time that would make it acceptable. I felt like giving up. How do I go on without someone I've been with my entire life? I never knew life without her. It's so easy to wallow in self-pity and hate everything and everyone but it is in those moments that you have to make a decision. You must decide that in life things don't always work out how you want them to, but that never stops God from using them for a good thing or allowing Him to give you something better. God doesn't change no matter how much your situation does.

On November 30, 1943, God sent an angel to this earth and on July 29, 2015, He called her back. Now, I can be angry that He took her away from me or I could be grateful and extremely humbled to know that for the first 20 years of my life, I trained under my guardian angel.

Our Testimonies

On behalf of everyone…Gran, I just want you to know that we love you and miss you so much. We will walk in your footsteps as we carry you in our hearts.

Thank you.

A Personal Relationship with Christ

Anonymous

This is a brief testimonial of my life before and after accepting Christ.

I was raised in a large family. I was the second youngest of a family of seven siblings and a troubled and warring mother and father. My parents held to Christian beliefs but unfortunately there was a strong disconnect between the affirmed and stated beliefs and actual Christian living. Christianity was more about rules and discipline than about a personal relationship with Christ.

As well, Christian examples and the fruits of the spirit were stretched pretty thin most of the time. This caused a lot of family dysfunction and turmoil. I was compelled to attend church regularly as a child but had never really been encouraged to have a relationship with Christ that I can remember.

The dysfunction in the family grew worse resulting in the divorce of my parents in my early teenage years. I became disillusioned about Christianity and angry with my family on many levels so I decided to leave home at the age of 16. My intention was to run away to the big city and make a new life for myself.

In the late 1960s I made my way from Alberta to Toronto and between the ages of 16 and 20 I indeed made a new and independent life for myself. I found good and secure employment and felt that I was finally free as a bird to just do whatever I pleased. I tried all the things that the world says are fun and for the time I had pleasure in them.

At the age of 20, I decided to move from Canada to Australia to live and work and was there for over two years. Then I decided to travel from Australia through various countries of the world for a period of one year. I ended up living and working in London, England, and there I reconnected with and married Jackie who I had known from my years of living in Toronto.

Jackie and I eventually came back to Toronto to live and continued to participate in a carefree go-with-the-flow lifestyle. Somehow, though, I always felt deep down a sense of emptiness and meaninglessness about life, and found myself searching more and more for truth and meaning to it all. I read many books about various religious and new-age beliefs.

This now being in the decade of the 1970s, there was much interest in the Jesus movement and that started to get my attention. I ended up purchasing a book by Hal Lindsay and Carole Carlson titled **The Late Great Planet Earth.** I believe that I was directed by God to purchase and read this book as up until then I never had much interest in Christian books, only new-age and other Far East religious books and philosophies. I think I always believed there was a Supreme God and that we were all flawed sinners capable of both good and evil, but was not clear in my mind about a divine purpose, outcome and destiny to it all.

However, after reading this book I started to understand what the plan of God was for humanity and this earth as prophesied in the Holy Scriptures about the first coming of Christ, His work of salvation on the cross for humanity and His eventual second coming and final redemption of all of His creation. I accepted Christ after reading the book but to be honest I did not fully understand a whole lot about true Christianity and faith. I started to attend a Bible-believing church and earnestly started to study scripture. Like most new Christians, however, I had many ups and downs in my faith, and my early Christian walk was challenged with old lifestyle habits, loss of old friends and various trials and tribulations.

My wife eventually came to faith in Christ a couple years after me. We experienced many tests to our new-found faith: we lost our first baby, then my wife was stricken with lymphoma cancer and had to undergo many radiation and chemo treatments. She was not given any assurance of overall recovery, just that there would be remission for a short period of time. This was a very hard test but we believed in prayer and miracles. My wife was anointed and prayed for and was healed. The cancer tumors in the lymph glands not only disappeared completely but she was diagnosed as cured and remains cancer-free to this very day. Looking back, I know that the losses, attacks and trials were directly from the evil principality and powers that we wrestle against as stated in **Ephesian 6:12**.

Over the years I continued to grow and mature in my faith but, of course, the Christian life continued to have its ups and downs and faith, its ebb and flow. The Lord eventually blessed us with another child and we dedicated and raised her up in the knowledge of the Lord. Today our daughter is married and I now have three beautiful grandchildren.

About seven years ago I started attending BFMC. My wife joined me in attending a little later and we have found the congregation to be both seekers and upholders of the truth as found in the Holy Scriptures. The people are wonderful, humble and gentle followers of Christ. I have, over the years, become very involved in helping to lead the Men's Ministry at BMFC. We currently have between 10 and 15 men who get together every third week to fellowship with praise and worship and then have lively Bible study/discussion on various topics. We, as a group of men, have also had the privilege and blessing to be invited to minister in song on a few occasions at seniors' facilities and also at church.

In summary, I would say that, yes, the Christian life and walk does have their daily challenges just as the Lord himself admonished us that it would in **John 16:33**. We go through times of joy and triumph but also times of sadness, weakness and fear. That being said, I can say with confidence as I look backward over my years as a Christian that God has brought me thus far as we read in **2 Samuel 7:18** and **1 Chronicles 17:16**. I also know with assurance that God has given me a living hope that He will make good on His promise to bring me and all who trust Him through to the very end as we read in **1 Peter 1: 8-9**.

With full assurance, gratitude and thanksgiving, I bless His Holy name.

Train up a Child in the Way of the Lord

By George W. B. Edwards

I am an only child of my mother who was a staunch Methodist, one who was involved in many activities in the church. So as a child, I accompanied her to church. She brought me up to follow in her footsteps. We rarely missed a church service on Sunday mornings at 11 o'clock and for me, Sunday School at 3 p.m., only to return to church at 7 p.m. for night service.

There were many times at night service I found myself nodding, wanting to sleep and my mother would whisper to me "stand up", fearing I would go into a deep sleep and have difficulty waking up. At the same time, she wanted me to be alert to listen to the sermon. Looking around I would see other children my age asleep with their feet on the bench and their heads on their parents' laps.

Growing up, it wasn't until I was in my late teens that I was allowed to go to the corner with the other children, and I remember them telling me that my mother had finally cut off the apron strings. I remember them telling stories about what happened at the corner, but I had no input because I was not there, so I could only listen to them.

I can remember one story. A lady in the village came to my mother and told her that I was teasing her mother when I passed. My mother being a district nurse (that is a midwife) in the parish of St. Paul's, was well known and respected. She was very upset and disappointed that I would tease an old lady or anyone for that matter, after her training that I should be respectful and polite to everyone, and never hit anyone first. But I knew I did not tease the old lady.

My mother took me by the hand and accompanied me to the complainants' home to apologize. A neighbour who was doing her laundry outside and who witnessed what took place came to my rescue. She said, "Nurse, it was not George, it was [this other boy]", calling him by name in the presence of the old lady's daughter, who then apologized to me and my mother.

Coming of age as a young adult, it was time to make a personal commitment to the Lord Jesus Christ and become a full member of the church. So I began classes and was later received into full membership. As a full member I served in the choir and later became a class leader. It was not long after that the sexton of the day retired and I was trained to do his duties, which included opening the church at 9 a.m., ringing the church bell for approximately 10 minutes (this was known as the first bell), and returning at 10:45 a.m. to ring the second bell, which was just before the beginning of the church service. For the evening service, I would return to the church at approximately 6:30 p.m. to prepare the lighting for the evening service.

Since there wasn't any electricity at that time, Coleman lamps were hung from the ceiling. These lamps had to be pumped occasionally to stay bright. At the end of the night service, the building had to be secured and all the equipment put away until the next week. This continued until my departure from Antigua to Canada.

When I was leaving the island, I was given the necessary referral documents to take to my new church. This was then the 1960s. Arriving and settling in Toronto, I took my documents to the Methodist Church on Shaw Street where Bishop Markham was in charge, and I was welcomed into full membership. After moving to Brampton in 1973, we (that is, my wife, three children and I) continued to attend church services in Toronto but only occasionally, due to the distance in travelling, especially in the winter months. We decided to worship locally at Central Park Baptist Church with the late Pastor Stanley Gompf. We also met Marva Williams' mother 'Mar' at the church. We met Joanne P. Belgrave, her sister, her mother and father who also attended that church.

In the late 1980s, Bramalea Free Methodist Church had an ad in the local paper about its services being held at Massey Street public school. So my family started attending and Rev. Carl Bull welcomed us. We attended there until we moved with Rev. Bull and the congregation to the new church, which is now our present location on 355 Howden Boulevard.

Before Rev. Bull's departure, he asked me if I would serve on the Board of Trustees, which I readily accepted. I've been active here at the church since then, serving in different roles. The boys were also active in the Sunday school and church until they moved on with their own family. My wife is also now a full member of the Church.

Some of my roles serving in the church include official board member, choir member, property management trustee, teller and usher.

Looking back over the years, I am very thankful and I give God all the praise and glory for my early childhood education, and for a mother who brought me up in the right direction. Some of her quotations to me were: "one is known by the company he keeps", "train a child in the way he should go, and when he grows up he will not depart from it". I tried hard to train my boys the same way.

I enjoy worshipping at the BFMC and assisting in the various roles. Because of this ministry, my faith has grown deeper and stronger in the Lord Jesus Christ.

A Prayer and Praise to My Heavenly Father

By Edith H. Edwards

Several years ago, I survived two car accidents: one horrifically in which my car was crushed but, fortunately, I still managed to exit on my own through the passenger's side, and walked away. The young man who ran the red light and hit me had to be pulled out of his car by three men.

Five years ago, I was very sick, diagnosed with diabetes and a blood clot in one of the lobes in my left lung. I fell unconscious. I went blind. I was not expected to survive. I was hospitalized in the Intensive Care Unit.

Lord, I love the way You often do what is unexpected. You saved my life. Your **Miracles** continue.

Lord, I know You have work left for me to do. I am open to whatever You have planned for my life. Lord, I know You have a music ministry for me. I am not a talented singer, but I like to sing, and someday I know I will be playing that piano.

Thank you, Lord, for not giving up on me. Thank you, Lord, for opening my ears to hear Your voice distinctly. Give me joy, precious Father, by bringing me to fellowship with these children in Sunday School.

Lord, I give You permission to hold me close and never let me go. Take complete possession of my life, Lord.

Thank you for the assurance of Your ever-present availability. I am grateful for Your strong and gentle touch. Lord, I will serve

You today because I love You. You have given me life. Thank You for not casting me aside. When the sun seems hot, Lord, You are my shade.

Lord, when the days of my life are over, I know You will be my Resurrection. Help me remember that there is life in You.

An Amazing Discovery

A reminder of God's faithfulness

By E. Gael Lohnes

Being inspired by another pastor's story of returning to his hometown at age 70, I felt a longing to do the same the summer of 2015. After 63 years, would anyone remember me? As a child of a country pastor I remember that we moved many times – but childhood memories drew me back.

I discovered that one church was demolished, another sold and a big new church on a hill replaced them. One kind postmistress called her elderly father who could tell me where my old school friends had gone – several deceased and others in long-term care. I thought "I am so blessed to have family and good health."

Arriving at Pembroke, Ontario, my husband and I searched diligently and found our old school, house and neighbourhood on a country road. Returning to our hotel we swam in the pool. A lady in the pool began talking with me. I told her the purpose of our trip – only to discover she was the granddaughter of my childhood neighbour who at 94 years old is very alert. He wrote a letter filling in a missing "puzzle-piece" of my life. This demonstrated to me God's amazing care of our family that year when both my parents were deathly ill and had difficult surgeries. At the time, I was nine and my brother was seven.

Where would we be today without God's amazing intervention then through our neighbours? My brother became a youth and music pastor (deceased at 28) and I a missionary. How could it be a coincidence that, in a pool in Pembroke, I would meet the granddaughter of the same neighbour who had helped us 63 years ago? Only God could orchestrate this.

The Day I Lost my Faith

By D. Monica Johnson

My niece was diagnosed with liver cancer. How could that be? She never smoked and was not around anyone who did. As a family, we started discussing ways to bring her to Canada so she could see a cancer specialist. My brother was consulting with a naturopathic doctor in Florida to find out what she could do to help.

Each time we called home, my sister would say, she (my niece) had had her off days but was generally feeling better. Our conversations with our niece were brief, but we thought she was just tired. One day, I was speaking with an aunt and asked how my niece was doing. She blurted out, "Your niece is dying." I had to take a seat. It didn't make sense. My sister, on one hand, was saying she was getting better and my aunt was saying something else. I told my husband, called the other siblings, and then I cried for a long time.

You see, this niece was like a sister. We had grown up together; I was only two years older than she was. It didn't even occur to the other four of us that she was a niece. And, she never wanted anyone to refer to her as a niece. That's why the news was so shocking.

We bought our airline tickets and left for Jamaica a few days after my aunt gave me the news. We realized she was ill, but we still had hope. We took turns sleeping in her bed to make sure someone was with her if she needed help. We spoke with her about everything, and her testimony was, "Lord, if I am the vessel through which my family and friends will be drawn closer to you, I am available, use me."

Three days later, on January 12, 2005, she passed away. That's the day I lost my faith. I quarrelled with God. I asked Him what He meant when He said in **John 13:14**, "If you ask anything in my name I will do it." I quoted **Matthew 7:7-8**, "Ask and it will be given to you...For everyone who asks receives..." But I was very bitter. For a year and a half, I could not pray. I was that mad with God. I thought of the life she lived, her generous heart, her silent suffering and yet she never complained. She hung on to her God.

In the midst of one of my rantings with God, I remembered her testimony: "Lord, if I am the vessel through which my family and friends will be drawn closer to you, I am available, use me." Did her testimony have a message for me? Yes, it did. Slowly, I turned back to God. I felt guilty at first, having not prayed to Him for so long, but He was ready and willing to forgive.

I lost my faith for more than a year. My doubts and fears took over my life. It was during a moment of reflection that my niece's testimony came back to me. That's what jolted me and drew me back to the God whom I had abandoned. It appears I had to lose my faith, go through the valley of doubt, in order to find God again. I am learning to depend on him more and more.

Dear Lord,

In moments when I lack faith, help me to remember that You keep your promises, and that "faith is the substance of things hoped for, evidence of things not seen." **Hebrews 11:1**

SPIRITUAL EXPRESSIONS IN POETRY, PROSE & VERSE

The ABCs of the Bible

By Yimika

The Words of the Holy Bible are precious and full of God's faithfulness and promises. Let the ABCs of the Bible come alive in your life for true redemption, salvation and the hope of eternal life.

A – Accept: Accept, Lord, the willing praise of my mouth, and teach me your laws (**Psalm 119:108**). Jesus encourages us to **ask** and it will be given to you; **seek** and you will find; **knock** and the door will be opened to you (**Matthew 7:7**).

B – Blessed: Blessed are the pure in heart, for they will see God. Blessed are the peacemakers, for they will be called children of God. Blessed are the merciful, for they will be shown mercy (**Matthew 5:8-9**).

C – Compassion: Because of the Lord's great love we are not consumed, for His compassions never fail. They are new every morning; great is your faithfulness (**Lamentation 3:22-23**).

D – Devotion: Serve God with wholehearted devotion and with a willing mind, for the Lord searches every heart and understands every desire and every thought (**Chronicles 28:9**).

E – Eternal: For God so loved the world that He gave His one and only Son, that whoever believes in Him shall not perish but have eternal life (**John 3:16**).

F – Faithful: No temptation has overtaken you except what is common to mankind. And God is faithful; He will not let you be tempted beyond what you can bear. But when you are tempted, He will also provide a way out so that you can endure it (**1 Corinthians 10:13**).

G – Grace: Because of His great love for us, God, who is rich in mercy, made us alive with Christ even when we were dead in transgressions (**Ephesians 2:4-5**). For it is by grace you have been saved through faith – and this is not from yourselves. The Lord's grace is sufficient for us, for His power is made perfect in weakness (**2 Corinthians 12:9**).

H – Holiness: Worship the Lord in the beauty of holiness (**Psalm 29:2**). Who is like unto you, O Lord, among the gods? Who is like you, glorious in holiness, fearful in praises, doing wonders (**Exodus 15:11**)?

I – I am: I am God, and there is no other; I am God, and there is none like me (**Isaiah 46:9**). Jesus said I am the way, the truth, and the life: no one comes to the Father, except through me. (**John 14:6**).

J – Joy: The joy of the Lord is our strength (**Nehemiah 8:10**). Shout for joy to the Lord, all the earth, break out in praise and sing for joy (**Psalm 98:4**). Worship the Lord with gladness; come before him with joyful songs (**Psalm 100:2**).

K – Kingdom: Seek first the Kingdom of God and His righteousness, and He will give you everything you need (**Matthew 6:33**). God's Kingdom is an everlasting Kingdom, and His dominion endures through all generations (**Psalm 145:13**).

L – Love: Love the Lord your God with all your heart and with all your soul and with all your strength and with all your mind, and love your neighbor as yourself (**Luke 10:27**).

M – Merciful: What does the Lord require of you? To act justly and to love mercy and to walk humbly with your God (**Micah 6:8**). Be merciful, just as your Father is merciful (**Luke 6:36**).

N – Nothing: I am convinced that nothing can ever separate us from God's love. Neither death nor life, neither angels nor demons, neither the present nor the future, nor any powers, neither height nor depth, nor anything else in all creation, will be able to separate us from the love of God that is in Christ Jesus our Lord (**Romans 8:38-39**).

O – Obedience: Walk in obedience to all that the Lord God has commanded us, so that we may live and prosper and prolong our days (**Deuteronomy 5:33**).

P – Peace: May the Lord of peace himself give you peace at all times in every way (**2 Thessalonians. 3:16**). As Jesus declared: Peace I leave with you; my peace I give you. I do not give to you as the world gives. Do not let your hearts be troubled and do not be afraid (**John 14: 27**).

Q – Quiet: The Lord is my shepherd, I lack nothing. He makes me lie down in green pastures, He leads me beside quiet waters, and He refreshes my soul (**Psalm 23:1-3**).

R – Rejoice: Rejoice in the Lord always, and again I say, rejoice. Let your gentleness be evident to all. The Lord is near. Do not be anxious about anything, but in every situation, by prayer and petition, with thanksgiving, present your requests to God. And the peace of God, which transcends all understanding, will guard your hearts and your minds in Christ Jesus. (**Philippians 4:4-7**).

S – Salvation: The Lord is my light and my salvation—whom shall I fear? The Lord is the stronghold of my life—of whom shall I be afraid? (**Psalm 27:1**)

T – Trust: Trust in the Lord with all your heart and lean not on your own understanding; in all your ways acknowledge Him, and He shall direct your paths (**Proverbs 3:5**).

U – Unity: Make every effort to keep the unity of the Spirit through the bond of peace **(Ephesians. 4:3).** The eyes of the Lord are on those who fear Him, on those whose hope is in His unfailing love (**Psalm 33:18**).

V – Victory: Thanks be to God! He gives us the victory through our Lord Jesus Christ (**1 Corinthians 15:57**). Everyone born of God overcomes the world. This is the victory that has overcome the world, even our faith (**1 John 5:4**).

W – Whatever: Finally, brethren, whatever is true, whatever is honorable, whatever is right, whatever is pure, whatever is lovely, whatever is of good repute, if there is any excellence and if anything is worthy of praise, think about such things (**Philippians 4:8**).

X – Xmas: Xmas as in Christmas. Joy fills the air as we celebrate the advent of Jesus Christ. For to us a child is born, to us a son is given (**Isaiah 9:6**).

Y – Yoke: Take my yoke upon you and learn from me, for I am gentle and humble in heart, and you will find rest for your souls. For my yoke is easy and my burden is light (**Matthew 11:29-30**).

Z – Zeal: Come with me and see my zeal for the Lord (**2 Kings 10:16**). Do not let your heart envy sinners, but always be zealous for the fear of the Lord (**Proverb 26:17**). The zeal of the Lord Almighty will accomplish this (**Isaiah 37:32**).

Dear Lord,

May the words of our mouths and the meditation of our hearts be acceptable in your sight, O Lord, our Rock and our Redeemer.

It Wasn't Much to Look At

By Sue Caldwell-Reed

It wasn't much to look at.
Just two pieces of wood. Cut, sanded, stained, attached together.
Wood, just wood. Not exotic. Just plain wood.
Mounted on top of a table pedestal. Top long since rendered useless by years of abuse.
Nothing much to look at.
Just a cross.

Each week that wobbly contraption was pulled out of storage.
Pushed and pulled, squeaking its protest at the action.
Hoisted, hauled and heaved
From dark storage to prominence,
Set on a stage. Just stood it there.
Just a handmade cross.

But it changed things.
Not an odorous gym any longer.
Now a church.
Not a just group of people
But a gathering of worshippers.
More than a handmade cross.

It was made from discarded material.
The pedestal abandoned, useless to most.

Sought out, reclaimed, refinished, redone.
Made into something we needed.
Made into a thing of beauty.
The Beautiful Cross.

Of itself it had no power,
It was just wood.
But that simple cross,
Made from rejected material
Turned our eyes from our humble surroundings
To the Lord of the cross.

It hangs now
In the church foyer.
Still a simple cross.
But reminding us that we come
Not for the surroundings
But to worship at the foot of the cross.

This piece of wood that was carved into a cross, hangs in our foyer and proudly welcomes all who enter our church.

Almighty God is Sufficient for Me

By Yimika

My God is sufficient for me – yes He is!
For He knew my name and formed me before I was born.
Yes, my God is adequate for you and for me –
Let the whole world know He cares for us.

His word is a lamp to my feet, and a light to my path.
He leads me besides still waters and restores my soul.
He redeems me from sin and makes me clean,
He sets me free, for who the Lord delivers, is free indeed.

Seek first the Kingdom of God and His righteousness.
Draw close to Him; be holy as He is holy.
Great is His faithfulness and His compassion fails not.
They are new every morning, great is His faithfulness.

The love of the Lord never ends! His mercies never cease.
His goodness and kindness know no bounds.
And blessed is the one who takes refuge in Him.
You are my defender and no weapons formed against me shall prosper.

You are my Rock of Ages, a sure defender that cannot be moved.
Even when the storms of life rage against me,
You calm the storms and anchor my faith in Your awesome power.
You deliver me from danger and protect me from evil.
You fill me with good things and renew my life.

My God is the Great I am.
He is the Beginning and the End.

Unchanging from everlasting to everlasting.
He is mighty to save and His name shall endure forever.

I am convinced,
Indeed, I am persuaded
That all things work together for good to them that love God;
That nothing can ever separate us from the love of God;
And His grace is sufficient for us.

Let the people of God praise His holy name; praise Him!
Let us worship Him and bow down before His throne; glorify Him!
Let the people of God say Amen and Amen.

Creativity

By Unita Sam-Darling

My mind feels full and bloated like a woman
      At the verge of giving birth.
      Is it a fertilized egg touched by the male sperm?
      Is it a divine-directed mind touched by the God of knowledge?

Or, is it a lonely woman's birth of fantasy?
      The verging of her malfunctioned, but regular
      Nature, moon directed but copulated by her own
      Thoughts, made full by constant heavy wonderings.

Is it a lonely mind full of much thoughts of this
      Pleasure, then pain, creating a farce of genius – of poetry?

      --- By their fruits you shall know them ---

Can you blame the apple for causing Eve's downfall?
      Eve, perfect mother, full of humanity stirring up in
      Her body, soul and mind.
What is she to do when nature calls directed by the great
      I Am – Jehovah?

Now tell me you great ones!

> Can we escape giving birth to our creativity – mind – body – soul?

When the great Creator, the great Yahweh said
>   Let us create man and his world.

Greatest union ever merged, God and His Word.

Explosion feel it, see it, in me, in you

>   --- Go and multiply --- do likewise ---

How then can I doubt for one moment the birth of my own creativity?

God's Love

By Unita Sam-Darling

I love you, you love you.

I still love you.

I give you all

Even my only son

You give me little

Or nothing at all.

That's God's love.

Learn to Depend on the Lord

By Iris Chang

Since Jesus came into my heart

I can depend on Him for all my needs

He has never failed me

All my trust is with Him

When you walk in His footsteps

You will never stumble or fall

He is always there to see you through

All the difficult times of your life

All we as believers can do is to trust in the Lord and we will have nothing to fear.

Sister Iris is over 90 years old

What BFMC Means

By Daisy Wright & June Rock

BLESSINGS

The Lord bless you and keep you; the Lord make his face shine on you and be gracious to you; the Lord turn his face toward you and give you peace.

Numbers 6:24-26

- **B**   Because He lives, we can face tomorrow.
- **L**   Lord, I lift Your name on high.
- **E**   Encourage each other with God's words.
- **S**   Sing unto the Lord a new song.
- **S**   Shout to the Lord, all the earth let us sing.
- **I**   In my distress, I will call upon the Lord.
- **N**   Nothing is too difficult for the Lord to do.
- **G**   God's grace is sufficient.
- **S**   So, I'll cherish the old rugged cross, 'Till my trophies at last I lay down.

FAITH

Faith is the substance of things hoped for, the evidence of things not seen.

Hebrews 11:1

- **F** Faith is a marathon; it's a test of your patience. Don't give up.
- **A** Amazing Grace, how sweet the sound that saved a wretch like me.
- **I** I believe in God, the Father Almighty, Maker of heaven and earth.
- **T** Trust in the Lord with all your heart.
- **H** Holy, Holy, Holy, Lord God Almighty.

MIRACLES

He has done all things well; He makes even the deaf hear and the mute speak.

Matthew 7:37

M   Mighty God, Everlasting Father, Prince of Peace. You are the great I Am and I thank You and praise Your name.

I   I can do all things through Christ who strengthens me.

R   Rejoice in the Lord always.

A   Ask and it will be given to you; seek and you will find; knock and the door will be opened for you.

C   Come to me, all those who are heavy laden, and I will give you rest.

L   Lo, I am with you always.

E   Even so, it is well with my soul.

S   Sweet hour of prayer, Sweet hour of prayer, that calls me from a world of care.

COURAGE

Be strong and courageous. Do not be afraid; do not be discouraged. For the Lord your God will be with you wherever you go.

Joshua 1:9,10

C   Count on God's blessings. He delivers what He promises.

O   Out of the depths of my heart, I cry unto you, O Lord. Answer me.

U   Under His wings you can safely abide.

R   Repent of your sins. He is faithful and just to forgive.

A   Abide with me, dear Lord, as You so faithfully promised.

G   Get down on your knees if you want the Lord to lift you up.

E   Enter into His presence with thanksgiving in your heart.

OUR CHURCH

BFMC – From Humble Beginnings

The following is a chronological account of BFMC and where we are today:

- 1980 – BFMC began in the spring of 1980 when Rev. Carl Bull, a pastor in the Free Methodist Church, invited a group of individuals to a Bible study.
- 1980-1982 – A group met at Lester B. Pearson Public School.
- May 2, 1982 – A congregation was established as a society of the Free Methodist Church.
- Late 1982 – The church began looking for other options due to a significant rental increase at Lester B. Pearson Public School.
- Late 1982 – Massey Public School became the new venue for worship.
- 1989 – Construction started at 355 Howden Boulevard.
- 1990 – The building was completed and dedicated in the fall of that year.
- 2016 – Mortgage paid in full.

Our Pastors

Over the past 34 years, BFMC has been served by nine pastors. They are:

1. Rev. Bruce Cryderman (wife Terri)
2. Rev. Carl V Bull (wife Sue)
3. Rev. Donald N Bastian (wife Kay) Bishop Emeritus of the FMCiC (Free Methodist Church in Canada)
4. Rev. Craig Peters (wife Marcia)
5. Rev. Felix Sung
6. Rev. Doug McLeod (wife Connie den Bok)
7. Rev. William (Rusty) Crozier (wife Sandy)
8. Rev. Keith E. Lohnes (wife Gael)
9. Pastor Dennis Ball (wife Christa)

BFMC – Community of Diverse People

By Yimika

After this I beheld, and, lo, a great multitude, which no man could number, of all nations, and kindreds, and people, and tongues, stood before the throne, and before the Lamb, clothed with white robes, and palms in their hands.

Revelation 7:9

Bramalea Free Methodist Church is a church that truly lives out its mission statement as *"A diverse people moving with one mind in cheerful, humble obedience to further the Mission and Kingdom of God in Brampton and beyond."* While this article focuses on the commemoration of Black History at BFMC, as a congregation we are proud to recognize the many cultures that form a part of the BFMC family.

The congregation comprises individuals from various countries, speaking a myriad of languages. These countries include: Antigua, Barbuda, Bangladesh, Barbados, Canada, Costa Rica, Dominica, England, Ghana, Grenada, Guyana, India, Jamaica, Nigeria, Philippines, Scotland, Sierra Leone, Singapore, South Africa, Sri Lanka, St. Kitts-Nevis, St. Vincent & The Grenadines, and Trinidad & Tobago. Such a rich culture has added to the diversity and fruitfulness of BFMC.

One of the celebrations over the past few years has been the commemoration of Black History Month (BHM) in February. This is a national event recognizing the contributions and achievements of Black Canadians, past and present, from all walks of life in the growth and development of Canada.

Our Church

It is important to note that the Free Methodist Church played an instrumental role in ending slavery by providing sanctuary for some of the early settlers in Canada.

As part of the Black History celebrations in 2016, the congregation, during a Sunday worship service, watched a depiction of Richard Pierpoint, a black Loyalist and true Canadian hero, and the contributions, determination and valour of black soldiers against strong odds, in the fight for Canada during the War of 1812. Named the Coloured Corps, this group of soldiers fought in the Battle of Queenston Heights, a decisive engagement with the Americans.

On another Sunday, we were inspired, informed and blessed with spiritual choruses and hymns sung to the pulsating African rhythm by the Krio Diaspora United-Southern Ontario (KDU-SO). This organization is composed of descendants of liberated Africans who settled in Freetown, Sierra Leone, and the surrounding villages, following the abolition of human trafficking in the mid-1830s. It is a story, narrated by David During, about "Binta", a young African girl snatched from her native home by invaders, and "John" (John Newton), the "wretch" that grace led to see the light in his famous hymn **Amazing Grace**.

As we rejoiced together, we once again reaffirmed that we are all one people created in the image and likeness of God who loves and cares for us. The experience was heart-warming, and many worshippers expressed their joy and hoped we could have similar celebrations in the future.

The celebration of BHM should not just be an annual ritual, but a pivotal event for Black Canadians to continue the process of integrating successfully into the Canadian society. We need to portray an accurate and complete socio-historical assessment of the pioneering events and contributions made by Black Canadians and to have their achievements recognized and articulated. We need to understand the social forces that have shaped and influenced our communities, hindered or promoted our capabilities, and to participate fully as equal citizens in the national development process. Black History Month reminds us of the struggles of the past, the resiliency of our people, past and present, and of our hope and determination for the future.

We all have a role and a responsibility to improve and sustain the spiritual as well as the material well-being of all Canadians. We need to rededicate ourselves to this task and to make a positive change in our streets, our neighborhoods and in our communities at large. In this regard, the church certainly has a primary and essential role to play in making this goal become a reality. In pursuing our vision and fulfilling our mission to carry the Gospel news in Brampton and beyond, we place our hope and trust in God Almighty, standing on His promises by faith. We pray that He will bless and guide us, and grant us the courage led by the Holy Spirit day by day, to have the joy and assurance of knowing and following Jesus Christ our Saviour and Redeemer.

Many Hands and Hearts Join in Fellowship

By Louis Isaacs

Bramalea Free Methodist Church over the years has seen many active committees and events which added richly to the fellowship and life of the church. Below is a synopsis of these achievements.

Outreach

The Outreach committee was established during Rev. Doug McLeod's tenure with the first chairperson being Audrey Isaacs and co-chair, Myra Watts. This committee spearheaded the annual multicultural event celebrating the diversity of the congregation. The theme was "Celebrating our differences through God's love."

The multicultural event featured flags of countries representing the diverse make-up of the congregation. In addition to the Canada's, there were flags from Antigua, Barbuda, Barbados, Dominica, England, Ghana, Guyana, India, Jamaica, Nigeria, Philippines, Scotland, South Africa, Sri Lanka, St. Kitts-Nevis, St. Vincent & the Grenadines and Trinidad & Tobago. The event also featured cultural dresses, national dishes and entertainment.

The second committee chair was Edna Fields, with co-chair Audrey Isaacs. The third committee chair was Jamila Liburd, with co-chair Lafleur Francois.

Outreach presence was evident at each Brampton Santa Claus parade for a number of years, distributing free hot chocolate,

Christmas story books and candy canes to citizens attending parades.

Bus shopping trips to the USA twice a year was part of the activities, with stops at the Festival of Lights in Niagara Falls on the Canadian side. The committee benefited financially from these shopping trips which allowed them to fund much of the events they initiated.

The Outreach Committee held yard sales from items donated by members of the congregation. The Easter Sunrise Service, which was usually followed by a sumptuous breakfast, was established as an outreach initiative and remains a current event.

Fundraising

The Fundraising Committee, chaired by Sherry-Ann Bedminister and co-chaired by Louis Isaacs, organized the annual 5k walk-a-thon, which left from the BFMC parking lot, went along Howden Boulevard to Chrysler Drive and back. Funds raised were used to purchase sport equipment for the youth as well as some musical equipment for the church.

Raising the Roof

The "Raising the Roof" event was spearheaded by Rev. Keith E. Lohnes at a time when the roof of the church needed to be replaced. In fulfilment of this initiative, individual pledges were made by the congregation. Another activity under the "Raising the Roof" program was a gospel concert organized by Christiana Nuamah, Marilyn Chang and Audrey Isaacs, which was held in the auditorium of Central Park Secondary School. This event was a success and featured well-known award winning gospel singer Marilyn O'Neil, the Zamora family singers of BFMC and our own Dave Reid with his **Reunion** group. After the roof was repaired, additional funds raised were used to tile the foyer and steps leading to the basement.

The committees and volunteers were diligent in their support to make these events successful.

Free-to-Serve Campaign

In July 2014, BFMC was without a pastor. In the months that followed, the church board concluded that before recruiting a new pastor, an accumulated debt needed to be paid. It was estimated that this could take more than a year. By February 2015 that debt stood at approximately $13,000. On the urging of retired Rev. Keith E. Lohnes, the Board agreed to undertake a "Free-to-Serve" campaign to eliminate this debt by the end of June 2015 – a daunting challenge at the time!

We urged our members to give over and above regular giving, trusting the Lord to provide. Some had doubts that we could reach the goal that quickly. With much prayer and God's help our members responded and by the end of May we had reached our goal. At the end of June, our target date, we had gone well beyond our goal, with a total raised of $17,995, more than enough to eliminate that debt, with the surplus going against our mortgage and enabling the church to proceed with securing a new pastor.

God is faithful!

Leading with Grace

By Audrey Isaacs & Jackie Piper

The Board is the governing body of the local church and it has been instrumental in keeping the congregation inspired through the changes and challenges we faced at BFMC.

The Free Methodist Church Manual states that the official board of the local church is responsible for the general supervision of its ongoing operation and all of its ministries. It plans for the organization and development of the church and its ministries. It has authority to recommend to the society proposals for major changes to the ministry and organizational plan of the church, and propose annual budgets or major changes to the budget. The Board also ensures that an annual performance evaluation of the lead pastor is done in accordance with the guidelines of the Free Methodist Church.

Our current Board comprises the following elected individuals: Audrey Isaacs (delegate/board chair), Dave Reed (alternate delegate), David Wright (board secretary), Jackie Piper (treasurer) and Sam Boison. On behalf of the members, these dedicated individuals meet once per month with the Pastor to discuss and fulfill the responsibilities entrusted to them. As a Board, we pledged to keep the congregation updated on all issues as they arise. Minutes from each Board meeting are posted in the foyer to inform individuals about the matters of the board and by extension, the church.

During the past two years (2013 to 2015), we went through a lengthy transition period without a pastor due to financial constraints. As Board chair, I would be remiss if I did not express appreciation to the members of the Board and ministry leaders for working together to keep all the ministries at BFMC moving forward during this time. Rev. Keith E. Lohnes deserves a special mention for providing continuity in leadership at BFMC and consistency in our pulpit supply roster. We also thank him for proposing to the Board and spearheading the "Free-to-Serve" campaign to raise funds to pay off the restricted funds owed, in order to allow us freedom to serve in ministry.

We have seen God's faithfulness in that we were able to raise more than the required amount of the "Free-to-Serve" goal. The excess funds were applied to the church mortgage. Thanks to you, the congregation, for your generosity in making this a reality. This enabled us as a church to move forward to employ a bi-vocational pastor.

Thanks to the dedication and hard work by the members of the Pastoral Leadership Task Force, on December 13, 2015, we were able to welcome Pastor Dennis Ball as our lead Pastor, his wife Christa and their family to BFMC. The Board is trusting in God that one day our resources will enable us to engage the pastor in a full-time position. It is with that in mind that the Board is looking to the congregation to continue co-operating with us and Pastor Dennis to make this arrangement work effectively.

Let's look ahead to where God will take us as a congregation in 2016 and beyond, to accomplish the mission He has given to us: *"A diverse people moving with one mind in cheerful, humble obedience to further the Mission and Kingdom of God in Brampton and beyond."*

Connections Team

By Joanne P. Belgrave

Give generously to them and do so without a grudging heart; then because of this the Lord your God will bless you in all your works and in everything you put your hand to.

Deuteronomy 15:10

Go out into the world and serve! Connecting Teams is a ministry to open up our hearts here at BFMC and help others in our community and beyond. God has placed it on our hearts to help our church family and others in our neighbourhood.

In the past years we assisted in helping families who were victims of fires and who lost loved ones. We lend a hand by cooking, caring and delivering food from our food bank. We also assisted the community by taking food to a local kitchen, and coats to women's shelters. In addition, we've put together gift bags of personal items and toiletries and delivered them to the shelters at Christmas.

When you think of others and place them first, God loves you for it and you will be rewarded. Not necessarily when you are looking for it but He will do so in His time. So always remember to give from the heart. It's a great feeling.

Keeping God's House Safe and Secure

By Sam Boison

The BFMC Facility and Property Ministry's mission is to manage and maintain all church assets in a manner that provides a safe and secure environment for our church and community.

The ministry helps with the maintenance of the property by our members who volunteer to help and serve with assigned maintenance tasks. Some of our responsibilities are:

- Inspect building property and equipment and prepare annual inspection reports
- Supervise and execute rental contacts
- Maintain an up-to-date inventory of all building equipment, appliances and furniture
- Submit the ministry's yearly budget
- Organize BFMC's annual Church Work Day
- Implement and monitor the security of all church assets
- Maintain and update a record of all security holders

Many of our members, at different times over the years, have volunteered to serve this ministry.

Women Active in Service

By Judith Sylvestre, Helen Charles and Edna Lawes

The Women's Ministry

Mission Statement: To empower and equip women of all ages to become Women of God so that we can create a nurturing community in Brampton and beyond where Christ can be seen.

The Women's Ministry comprises devoted women who provide spiritual guidance and support to families especially women in the church as well as in the community. As an extension of our Mission Statement, we believe that God has created each woman with a divine purpose and destiny.

The Women's Ministry meets on the second Saturday of each month, where they initiate and plan a number of activities to support deserving causes, and donate to charitable organizations.

An annual English-style Mother's Day tea party is held each May to celebrate mothers and mother-figures. Women have the opportunity to learn Biblical truths from experienced, spirit-filled contributors, and share their hopes, dreams, challenges and opportunities with each other. They help to build up one another and to strengthen faith, hope and trust in Jesus Christ.

One of the group's most memorable achievements was the baptism of five ladies following the study of Pastor Rick Warren's "The Purpose Driven Life".

Another amazing event was when the Women's Ministry hosted a one day seminar presented by **"IGNITE"**. **The purpose of**

"IGNITE" is to stir the passion in women and encourage them to be leaders in ministry. The group provides motivation, inspiration and training for this purpose.

Attendees listened to testimonies of the way God was using women, some in their broken state, to help others who could not help themselves. One of the testimonies was from a lady who was recovering from a car accident. Although she had no experience in the field of sewing she answered the call on her life to make blankets for children. With the help of others, she proceeded to make hundreds of blankets for shipment abroad. **Proverbs 31:30-31** says:

"Charm is deceptive and beauty is fleeting: but a woman who fears the Lord is to be praised. Honor her for all that her hands have done, and let her works bring her praise at the city gate."

Then, there was this other woman who created a chicken ministry, yes a chicken ministry! That ministry provides food for the less fortunate. Another mentioned how one can reach out to others just by taking that one small step across the room to connect with another person. Like the song writer said, "Step by step we are moving forward."

The members of the BFMC Women's Ministry regularly attend the "Springarama" Conference held every April in Kingston, Ontario, Canada. This Conference is sponsored by the Canada East Free Methodist Church, and each year, more than 400 ladies travel from various cities in Ontario to attend. The weekend gives participants an opportunity to learn, pray, praise and worship the Lord. It's also a time of giving and receiving smiles, laughter, and goodwill.

The BFMC Women's Ministry has been sponsoring a foster child in Haiti for a number of years through the International Child Care Ministry of the Free Methodist Church in Canada.

The Women's Hospitality Ministry

Mission Statement: To reach out in love by serving the people of Brampton.

The Women's Hospitality Ministry comprises dedicated women who assist in various ways to extend warmth and friendship to members of the church and to visitors. We believe and adhere to the fact that each individual is important to God. As **Hebrews 13:2** states, "Be not forgetful to entertain strangers, for thereby some have entertained angels unawares."

The ministry is responsible for hosting several functions during the year including the Christmas dinner, which is organized as part of our celebration honoring the birth of our Lord and Saviour Jesus Christ. This event is usually well attended by BFMC members and well-wishers. The program involves the singing of inspirational Christmas hymns and choruses, playing quizzes and word games, as well as enjoying an evening with relatives and friends. A variety of food, including a three-course meal, is served and guests have a chance to savour drinks such as ginger beer, mauby, sorrel and other beverages.

An annual Easter morning sunrise service is held in the parking area in front of the church. Members look eastwards as they view the majesty and brilliance of the rising sun. This brief ceremony has great significance as we reflect on the Crucifixion and Resurrection of our Lord. Members are treated to breakfast before attending Easter Sunday service.

The ministry organizes bake sales from time to time as a fundraising venture, and is also in charge of serving refreshments after Sunday worship service. Members take turns to prepare light snacks and hot beverages, which is most welcomed by worshippers. This period provides an opportunity for members to interact, share stories and encourage one another.

Making a Joyful Noise Unto the Lord

By Dave Reed

Worship is a 24/7 expression of honour, love and submission to God. It is an inside-out experience that should positively influence not only our own lives, but the lives of all we come in contact with. Guiding principles from scripture include love for God and others (**Matthew 22:36-40**), sacrificial commitment to renewed thinking and living (**Romans 12:1-2**), and a focus on the sincerity and integrity of our worship rather than on form or ritual (**John 4:21-24**).

The expectation for all who are involved in any aspect of worship ministry at BFMC is that these guidelines would be central in our planning and leading as well as our participation in worship.

The Worship team plays an essential role in the church and leads the congregation in singing during worship service. The team consists of those with a heart for God and who love to sing. Sunday after Sunday, this committed team, together with the worshippers, sing songs of praise and thanksgiving to God for His abundant blessings, grace and mercy to us.

Worship is a collaborative effort involving not only musicians and singers, but ushers, greeters, and those in the A/V (audio/visual) booth. Worship is also a participatory experience. Some years ago, during the Christmas and Easter festive seasons, interested members of the congregation were invited to join with the Worship team to practice and sing Cantatas such as **The Colors of Christmas** arranged by Marty Parks, **We Celebrate The King: A Christmas Worship Collection** arranged by Community Bible Church, and **Glory In The Highest – A New Hallelujah** arranged by Gary Rhodes. These projects spanned the range of styles from traditional to contemporary, and inspired all who participated.

We are hoping to increase the number of singers and musicians to bolster and enhance the performance of the team, and also to facilitate expanding our repertoire to incorporate more contemporary gospel songs and choruses into our worship as we seek to reach out to the youth and young adults. We continue to trust in God for His guidance going forward, that our corporate worship will glorify Jesus and enrich the lives of all those touched by this ministry.

SPIRITUAL KNOWLEDGE BUILDERS

Bible Word Search

Names of Prophets

By Isaac Burnett

Find and circle the names of the prophets listed below:

```
J  O  H  N  Y  S  I  E  K  U  L
S  O  M  A  A  D  A  M  I  F  A
J  Z  J  M  L  C  J  S  O  M  O
N  E  H  E  M  I  A  H  E  A  H
J  U  S  V  H  B  L  Z  A  T  N
A  P  M  U  A  O  E  E  U  T  A
C  E  A  N  S  K  V  R  D  H  U
O  S  R  U  I  S  A  A  C  E  H
B  A  K  E  L  E  B  A  H  W  S
B  U  L  M  A  H  A  R  B  A  O
J  U  D  G  E  S  E  S  O  M  J
```

ABEL	ABRAHAM	ADAM
AMOS	BARNABAS	DELILAH
ESAU	EZEKIEL	ISAAC
JACOB	JEHOVAH	JESUS
JOHN	JOSHUA	JUDGES
LUKE	MARK	MATTHEW
MOSES	NAOMI	NEHEMIAH
PAUL	RUTH	SAM

Biblical Anagrams 1

Based on Prophets

By Isaac Burnett

Unscramble the words below to reveal the names of well-known prophets:

NAROA	OSAM	ROBDEHA
HEILJA	AEHSIL	KHBKAUA
GIAHAG	OESHA	IJHMERAE
LHMIACA	CHAIM	SOEMS
THESRE	AHPZEHNAI	NSAMRO

Answers:

AARON, AMOS, DEBORAH, ELIJAH, ELISHA, HABAKUK, HAGGAI, HOSEA, JEREMIAH, MALACHI, MICAH, MOSES, ESTHER, ZEPHANIAH, ROMANS

Bible Trivia

Based on 'The New World'

By Isaac Burnett

Referring to your Bible, find the answers to the following questions:

1. According to **Genesis 1:8-20**, what kind of heaven is the air immediately above the earth?
2. According to **2 Peter 3:10–13**, what will happen to the firmament heaven due to sin?
3. True or False? The 2nd Heaven is found where the sun, moon and stars are located? (**Ephesians 4:10**)
4. True or False? The third heaven is not beyond the 2nd heaven? (**Ephesians 4:10**)
5. According to **2 Corinthians 12:4**, what does Paul call the 3rd heaven?
6. According to **Luke 23:43,** Jesus gave the dying thief an assurance of a place where?
7. True or False? God, His throne, and the Tree of Life are all not a part of Paradise? (**Revelation 2:7; 22:1-2**)
8. In **Revelation 1:8**, what two titles did God give to himself?
9. According to **Exodus 25:8**, what did God give his people instruction to build?
10. According to **Genesis 8:22**, what shall not cease as long as the earth remains?
11. Based on **Isaiah 30:26**, what shall be like the light of the sun?
12. What does **Isaiah 65: 21-25** say will happen to the animals?
13. According to **Isaiah 35:8**, what is the highway that leads to the Holy City called?

14. Based on **Luke 10:20**, what is the greatest honour given to man that should be a cause for rejoicing?
15. According to **John 8:44**, it is no wonder that God hates what?

Answers:

1. The Firmament heaven; 2. It will be destroyed; 3. False; 4. False; 5. Paradise; 6. In Paradise; 7. False; 8. He is the Alpha and the Omega (the Beginning and the End); 9. A sanctuary; 10. Both day and night; 11. The light of the moon; 12. They will live peacefully together; 13. The way of holiness; 14. That One's name must be written in heaven or in the Lamb's Book of Life; 15. Lying.

Bible Crossword Puzzle

By Yimika

This puzzle is based on names of persons, places and phrases found in the Holy Bible. Circle the correct names and words across and down.

P	E	T	E	R	A	J	E	T	O	T	I	T	H	E	R
A	F	O	M	I	C	O	M	R	I	H	B	E	O	V	E
U	R	G	L	O	R	Y	U	U	L	O	M	N	P	E	N
L	I	R	A	W	A	O	B	S	E	M	I	A	A	R	C
A	M	E	N	I	M	U	A	T	T	A	C	K	O	L	O
H	M	A	E	G	O	A	Y	E	E	S	A	U	P	A	U
L	O	T	F	E	S	T	H	E	R	R	I	N	E	S	R
I	C	A	D	N	I	L	E	W	N	A	A	N	D	T	A
G	R	A	C	E	C	A	A	X	A	G	H	A	E	I	G
H	A	M	L	S	O	S	R	T	L	E	B	Z	O	N	E
T	R	Y	O	I	N	E	T	A	O	N	O	A	H	G	R
Y	E	I	R	S	E	T	E	Q	L	D	I	R	A	T	H
D	A	W	N	Y	J	E	R	U	S	A	L	E	M	B	E
A	U	E	P	H	E	S	I	A	N	S	B	T	A	L	A
V	E	B	L	E	S	T	W	G	O	Y	A	H	T	O	V
I	F	T	O	A	U	R	B	O	W	A	N	X	T	H	E
D	I	V	E	R	S	E	S	T	D	L	G	V	H	E	N
E	G	I	F	T	A	G	E	N	T	L	E	N	E	S	S
H	B	E	O	S	O	G	G	Y	A	G	L	O	W	I	T

Answers

AMEN	ANGEL	ATTACK	BLEST
BOW	DAVID	DAWN	DIVERSE
ENCOURAGE	EPHESIANS	ESAU	ESTHER
ETERNAL	EVERLASTING	FIG	GENESIS
GENTLENESS	GIFT	GLORY	GLOW
GRACE	GREAT	HAM	HEART
HEARTS	HEAVENS	JERUSALEM	JESUS
JOY	LIGHT	LO	LOT
MATTHEW	MEN	NAZARETH	NILE
NILE	OH	OIL	PAUL
PETER	RAM	RARE	RIM
SNOW	TEN	TEST	THE
THOMAS	TITHE	TRUST	TRY

Biblical Anagrams 2

Based on Biblical Locations

By Isaac Burnett

Unscramble the words below to reveal the names of biblical places:

MARSAAI	ZARNAHTE	SARAECAE
MELJERASU	DAEUJ	THAYNEB
EEGLLAI	RINACTH	CEDMAAINO
ILIPIPHP	PHEEUSS	ETHSSAACINOL
UTARSS	OITHCAN	SMADASUC
EDALIPHALIHP		

Answers:

SAMARIA, NAZARETH, CAESAREA, JERUSALEM, JUDEA, BETHANY, GALILEE, CORINTH, MACEDONIA, PHILIPPI, EPHESUS, THESSALONICA, TARSUS, ANTIOCH, DAMASCUS, PHILADELPHIA

References

Bell Jr., E. (2011). *What are YOU Waiting For?* Pennsylvania: Bell Investment Group, LLC

City of Brampton (2015). *Community Gardens Information Handbook* [Online] Available at **http://brampton.ca**

Claudius, M. (1782). *We Plough the Fields and Scatter*

Crosby, F. (1873). *Blessed Assurance*

Crosby, F. (1875). *To God be the Glory*

Hall, E. (1865). *Jesus Paid it All*

Lehman, F. (1917). *The Love of God*

Lindsey, H. and Carlson, C. (1970). *The Late Great Planet Earth.* Grand Rapids: Zondervan

McGruder, C. (1986). *Thanks.* Rex Nelson Music Co.

Rankin, J. (1880). *God be with You till we Meet Again*

Scriven, J. (1855). *What a Friend we Have in Jesus*

Sykes, S. (1931). *Running Over, Running Over*

Unknown Author. *He's a Miracle Working God*

List of Contributors

The following is a list of contributors to **Conversations of Grace:** *Testimonies of Blessings, Faith, Mirales and Courage.*

The Children of the BFMC Sunday School (*Kingdom Kids*):

Arianna Estridge
Beth Zamora
Chrisna Zamora
Courtney Louis
Cheyenne Meme
Dakari Medwinter
Eriyana Powell
Eva Rose

Francine Twmasi
Gabryel Wasmund
Jaiden Belgrave
Janelle Gritter
Jazmin Duncan
Jazmine Rose-Brown
Jeremi Duncan

Jocelyn Belgrave
Jochebed Meme
Micah Gritter
Mirabel Meme
Naomi Rose
Quinton Louis
Ross Sunglao

Members and Friends of BFMC

Alex McFarlane
Anonymous
Audrey Isaacs
Bri-Anne Smith
Caroline Haynes
Christa Ball
D. Monica Johnson
Daisy Wright
David Reed
David Wright
(Pastor) Dennis Ball
E. Gael Lohnes
Edith Edwards
Eva Rose

Edna Lawes
Elsa Kelly
Esther Sarpong
Frances Ebun Wright
George W.B. Edwards
Helen Charles
Ida Chatham
Irish Chang
Isaac Burnett
Jackie Piper
Joanne Belgrave
Judith Sylvestre
(Rev.) Keith Lohnes
Louis Isaacs

Lynn & Henry Dyck
Maglyn Rose
Marcia Wright
Mella Rose
Monique Peynado
Ovid Wilson
Ronjel Stuart
Sam Boison
Sue Caldwell-Reed
Trevor Hitchman
Unita Sam-Darling
Veronica Crick
Yimika

The Big Bold Book Committee

Daisy Wright
Jasmine Rock

David Wright
June Rock

Isaac Burnett

Special thanks to Bishop Keith Elford, Bishop of the Free Methodist Church in Canada, for his review of **Conversations of Grace:** *Testimonies of Blessings, Faith, Miralces and Courage.*

Made in the USA
Charleston, SC
29 November 2016